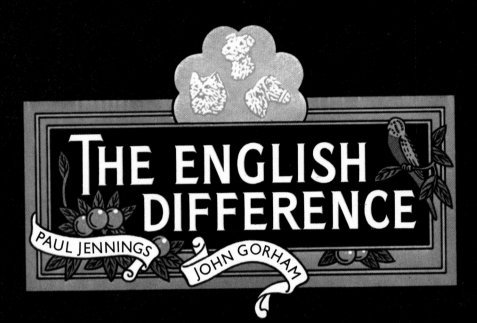

THE ENGLISH DIFFERENCE

PAUL JENNINGS · JOHN GORHAM

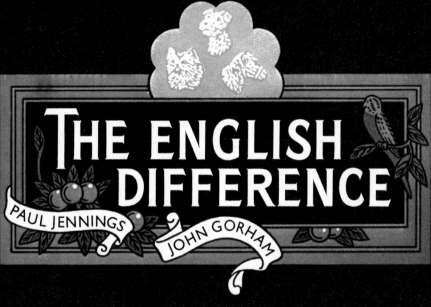

THE ENGLISH DIFFERENCE

PAUL JENNINGS · JOHN GORHAM

Words edited by
Paul Jennings

Illustrations & Design edited by
John Gorham

ISBN 0 904574 00 8

First published 1974 by
Aurelia Enterprises Ltd
7 Portland Place, London WIN 4HR

The layout and design of the book
were prepared in collaboration with
Ken Carroll

Printed in Great Britain by
C. J. Mason & Sons Limited

1

10 The Lie of the Land
12 Wild, on the Island
14 All the Fun of the English
16 Accustomed as we are
18 Local Architecture
20 Water
22 Country Town
24 The Village Fête
26 Writers' Regions
28 All Kinds of Gardens
32 Gardening Folk Figures
34 Grow It Yourself

2

38 Whatever Happened to Fang Managers?
40 Anyone for Yealming?
43 Unite in Love
46 Brass Bands: at Work and Play
48 On the Company's Ground
52 Top of the Bill at the Mechanics'
Institute

3

56 Interior Recollection
58 Shall I Wrap It Up?
60 Meat and Drink to Us
62 Now there are Plenty of Teaspoons
64 U'd Be Surprised

4

68 Popular Pleasures
70 Huntin', Shootin' and Fishin'
72 Odder Games
74 Come Out to Play
76 The Lyke Wake Walk
78 The County Show
80 The Sporting Weekend
82 Something about a Dame
84 On, On, On with the Dance
86 Pop
88 Make Mine a Pub
92 O, I Do Like
96 Singing is so Good a Thing
98 The Casual Look

5

102 The Haxey Hood Game
104 Bacup, and Other Dancers
106 Are You an Old Boy, Old Boy?
108 The Early Pearlies
110 Argent Threads Among the Or
112 Jollier Regalia
114 Pageants
116 Henley Royal Regatta

6

120 The Second Steam Age
122 Veteran & Vintage
124 Trams
126 Printed Ephemera
128 Machines for Museums

7

132 Not to Mention Brass Rubbings
134 What Does the Chef Recommend
this Evening, Barratt?
136 Bringing Jerusalem
138 Pet Theories
140 The Queen

 THE ENGLISH are vague people. As a whole they are always thinking about something else. This allows certain very un-vague persons among them to get away with all sorts of things which are not 'else' at all. 'Good heavens!' we said vaguely when we discovered that such persons had built dark satanic mills, and are now building dark satanic office blocks, 'look at those dark satanic mills; and look at these office blocks and urban motorways . . .' in much the same way as we said 'Good heavens, look at that Empire'. Lots of us had been thinking about trees, and gardens, and birds, and villages, our own landscape, all the time.

THE LIE OF THE LAND

FORTNIGHT or so on some baking Mediterranean beach is enough to start you thinking of the dear old English rain pattering down, though not so much perhaps of the waiting fog at Luton airport. In the First World War, men in their Egyptian tents lay on their backs in the darkness and longed silently to hear that so-called English sound again, borne upon a mild western wind, not on one of those mad foreign hurricanes or lashing monsoons, and for the smell of wet pavements, wet grass, wet everything. England's green and watery land, of springs and ponds, little winding rivers, fishing streams for small boys—polluted no doubt by now: but still so much is left despite all the savagery that has been expended upon it by motorways, developers, local authorities devoted to 'rateable values' and all those hard-faced men to whom Money is God: millionaires by the time they are forty, and dead at forty-five one would hope: 'grave men of sour complexion, money-getting men'.

One of the most crowded countries in the world, one of the most highly urbanized: but so much left almost untouched by the hand of Mammon, countrysides that have hardly changed for a hundred years. And for the discerning eye, landscapes that have not changed for five hundred or more years if you know how to read them as a surgeon can sometimes read the depths of the human body with his skilled eye and mind, and understand what has happened under the surface. Who would have thought, for example, that the vast cold horizons of the Fenland

of eastern England concealed 'one of the most completely recognisable ancient landscapes in Western Europe'? But so it is, though it takes the most highly-trained eye to perceive this buried scene. Or that that windy fortress of limestone rock known as Portland, jutting out into the English Channel off the Dorset coast, has just produced from a sheltered hollow on its leeward side (at Culver Well) the earliest evidence for settled farming in Britain, dating from Mesolithic times. We used to think of these makers of minute stone tools (microliths), older even than the Neolithic, as capable only of hunting and gathering natural food from the earth's surface or from the edge of the sea. Yet here, on the limestone floor, they had their primitive huts; and probably just beyond them their scrappy little fields—barely more than clearings from the natural scrub. There is nothing much to see: yet beneath our feet lies the evidence of the beginnings of farming, from some seven thousand years ago (c.5200 B.C.).

From such a simple beginning, and from others of similar age on the extreme western beaches of Cornwall, and inland on the Dorset downland and elsewhere, has evolved the immensely intricate knitted pattern of fields and farms, lanes and green tracks, hedgerows, ordered parks and great houses, thousands of villages, tens of thousands of hamlets, some twelve thousand medieval churches, and huge blobs of smoky towns known to the geographers as 'conurbations'. The whole of this vast and intricate scene has been hand-made, without the help of any power other than human strength and that of the ox until comparatively recent times. Thousands of years, hundreds of human generations, went by in this an-

onymous toil until the power of water was harnessed in water-mills in Anglo-Saxon times, perhaps in Roman times, mills that generated just about as much power at their best as a small motor car.

What I noticed about England, even when I was young, was its detail: there is so much to see, so little understood. The geological map is not just a map. Every change in its colouring is a change in the colour of the buildings in the villages all around, a change in the colour and the fertility of soils, even within a single field; a change in the texture of the village church from the mica-sparkling granite of the south-western churches through the pale blue lias of mid-Somerset, through a whole spectrum up to the Brontë-like blackness of the millstone grit of western Yorkshire: in time you learn from colour and texture where each of the hundreds of different stones comes from; and the names of the ancient quarries such as Polyphant, Beer and Purbeck, Box and Taynton, Weldon and Ketton, Clipsham and Tadcaster, and a host of others of local fame, ring in the mind like the bells of the ancient churches they were used for, where the village church can still muster a devoted band of ringers. 'Summoned by Bells' indeed: England is a country of church bells, not the monotonous clangour of foreign bells, but the melancholy pang-pang of the village church over the Lincolnshire marshland before evensong, the jolly peal of some town church that has kept its ringers, and above all the deeply-ordered clamour of cathedral bells over a city that has stood since Roman times, sounds that one's father, and grandfather, and great-grandfather heard long ago in their youth and in their stumbling old age.

The climate helps too, in creating this complexity, rainfall that ranges from some two hundred inches in the Lake District to about twenty around London; and the feel of the wind almost everywhere, though the prevailing direction may be wildly different: from the bitter easterly winds that the natives of Suffolk proudly tell you come straight from Siberia to the soft westerly winds of Devon where 'rain' is more usually called 'mist' as in Ireland, so soft and warming. Still, it is not a climate of great extremes: it is just small-scale like everything else. Micro-climates are important in England, as every gardener knows. Everything is on a human scale: no great deserts, no endless forests: England is closely packed, closely worked into many local patterns, hand-made for the most part by seven thousand years of human effort.

Over the western half and much of northern England the solitary farmstead or at most two or three small farmsteads clustered together are the typical form of human settlement. We don't even know how old the village is as a form of grouping: most bear Old English names, many have names of Scandinavian origin: the *bys* the *thorpes*, the *thwaites* and so forth and their origin seem obvious enough as the result of the Scandinavian conquest in the ninth century.

But place-names are a tricky kind of evidence: we know that Old English villages changed their names when a Danish or Norwegian landlord took over later: we also know that a fair number of villages with straightforward English names overlie yet older villages that existed just before the Romans came in the mid-first century, and some go back well into the Iron Age and survive for us to see. Best of all is Chysauster in western Cornwall, built of granite and later abandoned, perhaps because of a change in climate or more likely because the inhabitants moved on from an exhausted moorland site to fresh ground. In some fertile parts of England, on the other hand, it is quite possible that farming has not ceased since Bronze Age times (say 1800–1400 B.C.) and therefore that some nearby village was first chosen as a permanent site three thousand years ago, and has been built upon again and again, changing its name at long intervals. The village grew up as a group for mutual protection but mainly for co-operation in arable farming; the hamlet and the isolated farmstead are the product of pastoral farming from the beginning.

The field patterns of England have many different origins. Some date only from the large-scale replanning known as the Enclosure Movement (mostly between 1760 and 1850), though underneath them, usually visible from the air and sometimes on the ground as ridge-and-furrow, lies a much older field pattern. At the other extreme of age are the tiny, granite-walled fields of western Cornwall and most of Wales, fields that have not changed their size and shape since they were first made in the Iron Age (say from 500 B.C. onwards) for in a windy climate shelter was vital to the stock, and tiny fields hacked out of the scrub and bracken with primitive tools are still just right for this kind of farming.

It is now possible to date unmanaged, unkempt hedges with a reasonable degree of accuracy. Work by Dr Hooper of the Nature Conservancy has shown that the older the hedge the more complex and varied is its vegetation; and more than that, that roughly speaking the number of shrubs and trees in a sample length of hedge represents the age of the hedge in centuries; one new species having colonized itself every hundred years.

The land was originally cleared by large-scale burning in early days; later as land became relatively scarcer, by a more careful hacking with axe and mattock. Even

so England and Wales still keep a million and a half acres of common land, most of it high moorland but, remarkably, much of it lowland like the well-known commons in and around London or, farther out, the quiet brown heaths of eastern Suffolk just back from the sea. Land that has never been tamed even after thousands of years.

What else do we miss when far away from our native England? It is the trees, the constant flickering of birds along the hedgerows, and the church spires and towers every mile or two at the most, rising from the clustered full-grown trees. There are no great forests except the artificial creations of the Forestry Commission, but our hedgerows have for centuries been studded with ancient trees such as the elm and the oak, so native to our landscape that some of our rivers were named after them when men first set eyes upon a nameless stream. The ash is another old tree in the landscape: many English villages and hamlets are named after it. The beech is also of immense antiquity in the scene; but the honeyed pomp of the sycamore, so redolent of northern moorlands, only came into the picture in Elizabethan times, mainly to act as shade and as a wind-break in a harsher climate than that of the lower ground.

England is rich in small birds: how silent and lifeless the landscapes of other countries seem, not merely because foreigners have no scruples in shooting everything edible in sight but also because there is so little cover. The mileage of English hedges is almost unbelievable: in ten Devon parishes alone in the 1840s there were just under eight thousand miles of hedgerow. The fields were tiny, still unchanged from the hand-made intakes of the Saxon or medieval peasant; but even then the big landowners were destroying hedges on a considerable scale in the interests of better farming. So many fields were too small for even the smallest of the newly-invented

farm machinery; and now, with huge machinery as big as weapons of war, we are going far too far: destroying many thousands of hedgerow-miles a year, and with it an infinite number of birds and small wild life. We are creating 'dust bowls' for the first time in our history in the interest of the Barley Barons who mine the soil in this generation and will leave it exhausted in the next. Those East Anglian fields that stretch to the far horizon; barren of trees and hedges, broken only by a few towering pylons and perhaps a mess of factory-farming buildings that are worse than Subtopia.

Trees go at the same rate, helped by widespread disease of elm and ash. There are many such melancholy scenes once rich in natural life, and in human life; for the new machinery means that the English fields look so empty of people too—just one man sitting on a huge machine, polluting the air all round him. One thinks of the Bavarian fields, still looking a good bit like Tudor England, busy with men, women and children. 'A fair field full of folk': once it was true of England, but no longer. And our churches, once so thick on the ground, decay and we are warned away from the danger of falling masonry. So much to lament over.

Yet for those who know their England there is still so much to see, solitary places like the Breckland, or the old sheep ranges of the northern moors once colonized by Fountains and Bolton and other famous abbeys, or the ancient bastion of Portland where one look at the two-and-a-half-inch map is enough to set one off at once.

To the historian it has all happened before in some form or other: the times are evil, but there are plenty of escape routes yet. Nature will one day take over again when the Barley Barons and the sour-faced Developers are dead, buried, and forgotten.

W. G. Hoskins

WILD, ON THE ISLAND

NGLAND is different; of that there can be no doubt but just what makes it different depends upon who you are, or where and what your upbringing. Standing upon the eastern side of the North Sea the wildlife of these offshore islands seems but a pale reflection of the variety that exists upon the continent of Europe but, being kind to those apparently less fortunate than themselves, the Continental biologists will readily concede it is not the fault of the English who love wildlife more than most. The paucity of species, they say, is caused by our small size and the separation from themselves by the narrow strip of water we call the English Channel.

In turn, across the sea on the western side the Irish place a blessing rather than the blame upon St Patrick and not upon their size and sea—noting especially an absence of snakes from the Emerald Isle.

An Englishman, of course, has answers for such comments: he cannot understand why St Patrick, as a true patriot, along with snakes should banish the harvest mouse and mole, the beautiful Herb Paris and Lilies of the Valley from the woods, Scabious and Restharrow from the pastures or the Milkvetch from the scrublands of Ireland.

To a European the Englishman will indicate that this one small area is a focal point for the wildlife from both north and south. The Englishman has the Wild Madder and Tutsan from Spain and the Mediterranean along with the Hornbeam from central Europe, which neither Spain nor Norway has. He has Sweet Gale from the Atlantic and Baltic coastlands which central Europe lacks; and given half a chance a botanist truly Britannic will wax lyrical about his remarkable collection of mountain plants, citing Dwarf Cornel, the Cloudberry, Mountain Avens, Starry Saxifrage, the Alpine Ladies' Mantle, but will carefully forget that the rarest of these in England, the Bog Sandwort, is neither pretty to look at nor particularly rare on the continent of Europe.

An insular zoologist would make the same remarks of his own speciality: an ornithologist would quote the forty kinds of bird found in our islands and nowhere else, only to be answered from the Continent that none of these forty is more than a subspecies and that there are no real species peculiar to the United Kingdom. If our ornithologist were inclined to argue he might get away with the Red Grouse. But the Continental would regard this as just a racial form of his own Willow Grouse. Even accepting the Continental

view of the grouse's status, the less argumentative British ornithologist can still console himself with a larger number of races than any other European country of comparable size.

In a like wise the ardent patriot ichthyologist would speak of eight species of Coregonid fish confined to Great Britain, and the mammal man (and there are such specialists; there is in fact a Journal of Mammology) of subspecific variations peculiar to this country, of the Bank Vole and perhaps the even more numerous forms of the short-tailed vole and the long-tailed field mouse, though to preserve these as 'English' the patriot must continue to consider Scotland a subjugate nation.

An academic biogeographer isolated from patriotic feeling and owing allegiance only to his ivory tower of learning would admit the differences and fit them in to a general theory. Such a theory should explain the differences between the mainland of Europe and the offshore islands called the United Kingdom but to be general should also explain the differences between all such archipelagoes and their mainlands. It can be done.

The differences between island and mainland are of two kinds: on any island there are fewer species than on the mainland and in any species living in both places the population on the island tends to be slightly different from that on the mainland. The first difference has, at first sight, an obvious cause—any offshore island will be smaller than the mainland and hence have less room for plants and animals. However, the difference goes deeper than this, for islands not only have a smaller total number of species upon them but also a smaller number of species per unit area than the mainland. This would not have been so when England was physically joined to Europe. Then equal areas in England and France would have had equal numbers of plants and animals; there would have been no English difference. Once the Channel was formed, however, the populations of wildlife in England cut off from France must have suffered many vicissitudes and some died out or were killed, like the beaver and the wolf. If the Channel hadn't been there England might have been recolonized more easily and the numbers maintained. Despite the Channel colonists have arrived like the rabbit or the pheasant. Hence the number of kinds of plants and animals existing on an island depends on a balance being struck between the rates of two processes, extinction and colonization. The rate of extinction will depend mainly upon the size of the island and the amount of room allowed for wildlife since the smaller a population the more likely it is

to become extinct while the rate of colonization will depend upon how far the island is from the mainland. Therefore we can begin to understand why France has more species than England and why Ireland has fewer. Thinking on the same lines can also produce reasons for the second kind of difference: the differences between populations of the same species living on an island and on the mainland. There is a good chance that a new colonist from the mainland, which succeeds in founding an island race, will be different from its siblings which remain at home; it will at least be more adventurous. There will also be fewer individuals making up the populations on the island, so to some extent inbreeding must take place.

So, by being different to start with and by inbreeding, a really isolated, small population will obviously be different and this is probably why there are distinct races of short-tailed vole and long-tailed field mice on the Hebridean islands or distinct races of the Vendace in isolated lakes and lochs.

However, even if the colonist is no different the subsequent generations may become so since so many competitors will be left behind on the mainland and new situations for feeding and breeding will be available on the island. The island population will evolve into a distinct race to take advantage of these new situations. Different the wildlife may be and the English may pride themselves on their Chough or Twite but the island condition is shared by others. Even Sardinia has its own Meadow Brown butterfly!

This is, however, an Anglo-Saxon attitude and it is indeed in his attitude to wildlife that, to an Englishman, lies the cornerstone of the English difference. The English think they like wildlife though it is hard to find evidence to prove the case for the English against Continental countries. The first Swiss national park was declared in 1914, Spain had two in 1918, yet it was not until after the Second World War that the British Government took action. Admittedly Western Germany still has no federal system, only highly variable provincial laws, yet 4 per cent of their population holds membership in a nature protection society, in Britain it is less than 1 per cent, about on a par with Sweden, yet again in Sweden over 5 per cent of the land surface is protected but in Britain it is less than 1 per cent, none of which argues a devotion to wildlife greater than that held by a European. Only a true Englishman can see beyond such official statistics—wildlife in foreign countries needs protection, English wildlife is different, it doesn't. Being English is sufficient insulation in itself.

Max Hooper

ALL THE FUN OF THE ENGLISH

CHOOSE any sizeable travelling fair and you'll discover a little of England's history.

You'll find the heroes and heroines, the fads and the fancies of the last eighty years; ways of life that have long since passed and fashions that have faded.

You'll find Mickey Mouse and Winston Churchill, pin-ups and Teddy Boys rubbing shoulders with Queen Victoria. Astronauts, GIs, speedway cyclists and Edwardian principal boys mingle under banners crying 'Have a Go Joe' and 'It's a Gas, Man'. While the old Esso Tiger still leaps from the rounding boards.

You'll see ultra baroque carvings and mirrors fit to grace the most splendid Edwardian music-hall, air-brushed art deco and 'futuristic' designs and next door the chromium and flashing lights of the latest rides.

And it's all wrapped in a heady mixture of the top ten and organ melodies of yesterday.

If ever there was an art form created by the people for the people, this is it.

A lesson in effective communication, if you like. Because, like the packaging of a bar of soap, fairground decoration has a job to do. Each stall, booth and ride must compete to attract the public and win their custom.

So next time you see the lights and smell the hot-dogs, look around for a few old friends. They're not far away.

Geoff Weedon

STALIN

ACCUSTOMED AS WE ARE

FOR Bottle-kicking and Hare-pie Scrambling on Easter Monday at Hallaton in Leicestershire, the rector cuts the hare-pie before the muddy task of kicking small casks of beer from Hare Pie Bank begins.

2. St Ives, Cornwall, celebrates Feast Day in early February by Hurling the Silver Ball. The mayor tosses it to the crowd and it is thrown about till noon, no player retaining it for a moment longer than is necessary.

3. At Hocktide, after Easter, in Hungerford, the crier sounds a horn, tutti-men, carrying tutti-poles decked with ribbons, nosegays, and an orange, go round demanding a kiss or a coin (with a ladder, to reach upstairs windows), accompanied by an orange scrambler carrying a sack of oranges.

4. On Lady Day (25 March) in Halstead, Essex, a pewter spoon is thrown into the air to be scrambled for by the wiggy boys, so called from their traditional straw caps.

5. For the Ascension Eve Penance at Whitby, Yorkshire, a 'Penny' (penance) hedge of stakes and boughs is built at the sea's edge, and it must be strong enough to outlast three tides. This yearly task is said to have been imposed by a twelfth-century abbot after a priest was killed by huntsmen. At the conclusion the mayor's bailiff sounds his horn and cries 'Owte upon they!' in condemnation of the impious slayers.

6. Every Good Friday at the Widow's Son inn at Bow, in the East End of London, a bun is dropped by a sailor into a basket suspended from the ceiling. . . .

There are so many old customs in England, and many of them sound so extraordinary in the age of hovertrains and lasers, that anyone with a pass mark in Elementary Satire (First Year) could make up seemingly genuine ones. In fact, only one in the above list is a pure invention (Guess? It is No. 4). But the others are all perfectly real. Folklorists and old custom collectors will know which they are, but to most readers, it won't matter. England has a thousand old customs not least because a thousand years have left them free to grow, unmolested, deep-rooted, unquestioningly accepted; the kind of thing which, like children's games, has a mysterious handed-down life of its own—indeed it is just possible that we may see the ultimate paradox. Once written and scholarly attention, let alone the searchlight of the mass media are turned on them, they may at last die in the face of modern scepticism, modern embarrassment at any ritual and symbolism, modern *dreariness*.

Take the Lady Godiva procession, for instance. Coventry is a mysterious, Saxon town. In the thirties people worked at the Coventry Gauge and Tool, or performed basic, nameless mysteries of metal smithery in the Coventry Swaging Company; articulate with their hands, not with words. At the hub of a vast immigrant population of Irish, Geordies, Scots, Welsh, there were these few hundred silent, lantern-jawed, prodigiously skilled tool and jig makers, setters-up of factories for less-skilled men. Yet from their secret past came not only the Coventry Miracle Plays, and that most haunting and plaintive of lullabys, the Coventry Carol, but also a symbol as basic as any of those rediscovered in Greek literature by Freud, such as Oedipus or Electra; the inviolate naked woman, fearful and innocent— Lady Godiva.

Before the war, she appeared, the

decorous tights-clad star pupil of some local riding school, every few years in the hospital carnival procession. Nowadays we are all Peeping Toms, with our strip clubs and a National Theatre literary adviser who also was responsible for *Oh, Calcutta!*: and perhaps fears that the citizenry would no longer be as restrained as they were in the original legend are responsible for the fact that she has only appeared twice since the war; for the Festival of Britain (1951) and, who would have thought it, the Coventry Cathedral Festival in 1962.

This, of course, is a classic example of something that has happened throughout such Christianization of this island as was ever achieved; the church giving its blessing to something eternal (pre- or post-Christian, who can say?) in man. Wells and water have always been sacred, mysterious, and you could find in many

astern countries some sort of link with
e nevertheless unique Derbyshire cus-
m of well-dressing.

The most famous of these wells, at
issington, used to be decorated on
aundy Thursday, and various explana-
ons were offered; its pure water had
ven comparative immunity, from the
lack Death, once there was a drought
verywhere except *at* Tissington, and so
n. But the more obvious fact is that
erbyshire is a very *mineral* sort of
our.ty, and it's this symbolic conjunction

tiny nails, and there is never any lack of
people to do the many jobs, with a curious
handed-down skill (the flower petals go in
last, and in such a way that rain will run
off one on to another, not into the clay,
thus softening it). There is obviously a
resurrectional, spring association, but
nowadays well-dressing is spread through
the summer. Wirkworth's is on Whit
Saturday, Youlgreave's is on the Saturday nearest to the Feast of St John the
Baptist, Eyam's is the last week in
August.

pounds, for their famous Horn Dance,
which takes place on Wakes Monday—
the Monday after the first Saturday after
4 September. The biggest pair of those
used for many generations weighs $25\frac{1}{4}$ lbs.
and has a spread of twenty-nine inches,
and even the smallest are $16\frac{1}{2}$ lbs. and
twenty-nine inches. Wearing these mon-
strous things, six men in Tudor costume,
together with others as Hobby Horse,
Maid Marian, Robin Hood, the Fool, the
Musician, start at 8.30 and with numerous
stops, complete a dance of fifteen miles
by 8 p.m.

The Helston Furry Dance in Cornwall
is not furry at all, since the word comes
from the Latin *feria*, (a holiday), and
before it starts, people bring in green
branches and sing that they have brought
the summer. In Wishford Magna and
Grovely, near Salisbury, people go out and
fetch the largest green branch that can be
carried by hand, and there is a procession
led by the band, a man with the Union
Jack, four women with sackcloth aprons
carrying faggots on their heads, and
people in fancy dress; but the most
prominent thing is the banner saying
GROVELY. GROVELY. GROVELY.
AND ALL GROVELY. UNITY IS
STRENGTH.

Well, it is, and it is something deeper
than a paper abstraction. It has to do with
a *place*. Even today there are remarkably
few embarrassed smiles in Castleton
(Derbyshire again; Derby, where they
make Rolls-Royces, not all that far away)
when a man in Restoration costume,
almost smothered by the Castleton garland, a conical framework of flowers with
the 'Queen Posy' at the top, rides with his
queen following side-saddle, and band
playing the Garland Dance, to the church
on to one of the eight tower pinnacles of
which the garland is subsequently hoisted.

Nor is it thought extraordinary that at
the law courts, on or near 21 October, six
horseshoes and sixty-one nails are given
to the Queen's Remembrancer by the City
Solicitor (acknowledged by the words
'good number') as quit-rent of a forge that
once stood where Australia House now
stands. After all, this has been going on
since before anyone knew there *was* an
Australia. Meanwhile, on 11 November,
down at Fenny Stratton, they fill six
bulging little cannons with gunpowder
and blast them off at hourly intervals;
they're called the Fenny Poppers. Quite
recent, as old customs go; the whole thing
dreamt up by an eighteenth-century
rector. What will be interesting will be to
see whether the New Towns like Steven-
age, Harlow and Milton Keynes start
developing a few old customs (after all,
the Dagenham Girl Pipers, surprisingly
issuing from that unprepossessing Essex
town, were an example of instant tradition). One thing is certain; they won't be
properly English until they do.

Paul Jennings

of water and rock that makes one see how
rightly Biblical resonances tune in with
this lost-in-antiquity old custom.

It is curious how the actual designs,
which are strongly reminiscent of the very
representational but slightly wishy-washy
Bible pictures in Victorian elementary-
school classrooms, take on a real folk
vitality because of the mosaic method of
using flower petals, bits of fluorspar, pine
cones—'anything natural' is the criterion.
The design is pricked on to an inch-thick
panel of clay held in place by hundreds of

Well-dressing has got into British
tourist literature now, but it isn't preserved purely for tourist reasons. When
you are on the spot the thing has a kind of
unquestioned vitality of its own. One of
the keenest helpers in the well-dressing at
Ashford-in-the-Water is a lady who was
born in Bexhill, Sussex, worked all her life
in London, and only moved to Derbyshire
on retirement.

The people of Abbots Bromley, Stafford-
shire, recently acquired six *duplicate* sets
of antlers, each insured for one hundred

LOCAL ARCHITECTURE

THE GREAT, the unique thing about local architecture in England is that it isn't only tremendously local in place; it's local in time as well (although of course many buildings have grown almost like trees, and it is perfectly possible to go through a modern porch, through a Victorian kitchen into a Georgian dining room and up some Georgian stairs into a Tudor bedroom).

No doubt geology has something to do with it. There is no stone in East Anglia, indeed in all the south east; therefore churches are of flint (there wasn't any real domestic architecture until Tudor times; what we now think of as a 'cottage', with roses round the door, was originally the dwelling of a fairly substantial yeoman, of the new class that emerged after the Black Death, halving the population in 1350, had led to scarcity of labour, the breakdown of the rigid feudal system, and above all the low-labour, high-profit sheep-farming and the wool trade that founded our prosperity; not for nothing does the lord chancellor still sit on the Woolsack).

There is a stone belt running from the Severn estuary to that of the Humber. In the north and west you may see old houses built of 'cob' which is a kind of mud cement invented many centuries ago (and often painted white, which became a fashionable exterior colour in the eighteenth century, when even if you had mere bricks it was smart to cover them over with stucco.) In St Bees (Cumberland) there are still houses with walls $2\frac{1}{2}$ feet thick; actually two outer walls of stone, the inner space filled with rubble from the beach.

Until the Georgian period (which was

our own highly individual twist, with infinite variations on fanlight, window, scroll, porch and roof, on the strictly classical themes of the Continent's Renaissance) a fair amount of English building development and experimentation took place in wool-rich East Anglia, once our predominant trade side, before we had wider, Atlantic views. In a place like Lavenham in Suffolk you can see classic examples of the huge-timbered 'jetties' known locally as 'oversails', where the second storey is wider than the first, so that its weight steadies the long, heavy beams of the ceiling. Shortage of timber towards the end of the fifteenth century led to simpler designs; a beam down the middle of the ceiling into which cross-beams were tenoned, and the construction

of the house round a simple frame (known as a 'balloon' although really it was more like that of a square airship) the spaces filled with wattle-and-daub. Later this timbered style leapfrogged across the stone Midlands to Cheshire and Shropshire where it reached a black-and-white final glory. But we hadn't finished with wood weatherboarding to keep the driving rain and east wind out (incidentally, it was only gradually that we stopped building houses facing north as the idea died hard that the plague, which had started in Dorset, was borne on the south wind or else they would face east or west so that the south wind could only blow at the blank end of the house). The south east and Thames Valley varied this with tile-hung walls.

After the Civil War came better roads, and wagons. The piled-up, medieval towns of jettied houses gave way to the great Georgian period; chimneys, the great status-symbol of Tudor and Jacobean times, put in the centre of farmhouses with the rest built round them, returned to outside walls. Victorian times brought high rooms (because of gas fumes), and a great argument between 'pure' classical Greek, and Gothic revival; not to mention delicious cast-iron verandahs and curlicues. Things are more standard now; even so, more than any country in the world, England is the one where you could be put down blindfold in any district and, after wandering round for a mile or so, tell from the houses *what* district it was.
Paul Jennings

WATER

THE ENGLISH are obsessed with water, or rather its emotive and aesthetic attributes as distinct from their necessitous requirements. We have plenty of it in nature, liberally distributed in lakes, mill-ponds, rivers (in a rich variety of qualities), streams (swift-flowing mountain sparklers and sluggish dawdlers across our plains) and every form of man-made contrivance ranging from vast reservoirs in remote mountains down to mini-fountains in suburban gardens with electrically propelled jets (sometimes illuminated by coloured lamps at night) squirting into small, concrete basins in which loll two or perhaps three goldfish. Supreme in our aqueous world is the Lake District, where we have mountains surrounding a variety of naturally formed sheets of water, which today are at times scarcely visible for the crowds of admiring holidaymakers, sight-seers and motor vehicles.

Earlier generations, however, did not have this present enthusiasm for this watery district. In 1624 was published *A Relation of a Short Survey of 26 Counties*. This describes the Lake District so: '. . . nothing but hideous hanging hills, and great Pooles, that in what respect of the murmuring noyse of those great waters, and those high mountainous tumbling rocky Hills a man would think he were in another world.'

A sentence from John Dryden's 'Indian Emperor' of 1667 also suggests the displeasure with which the English looked on, or perhaps more accurately, thought about such scenery as we now admire: 'High objects, it is true, attract the sight, but it looks with pain on craggy rocks and barren mountains.'

A century or so later all had changed. For the young gentry it had become the fashion to gallivant around Italy and appreciate the echoes of classical art. So in 1776 we get William Hutchinson writing: 'The paintings of *Poussin* describe the nobleness of Ullswater; the works of *Salvator Rosa* express the romantic and rocky scene of Keswick, and the tender and elegant touch of *Claude Lorraine*, and *Smith*, pencil forth the rich variety of Windermere.'

But well into the eighteenth century, the Englishman's love of water still demanded that to please him it should be cabin'd and confin'd into geometric figures or ingenious tricks in the manner of the French garden designers such as Le Nôtre had taken over from the Italians. In 1712 John James, the architect of St George's, Hanover Square, published a very accurate English translation from the French of d'Argenville's classic work published three years earlier on French gardening.

Of its seventeen chapters, two only concern water. The first discusses the methods of searching for it and, when found, conveying it to the garden. The second concerns the design and craft of making fountains, basins and cascades of water. There is no reference to sheets of water.

The 'basins' are the nearest approach—small geometrical shapes, covering areas no greater than a parterre, though the pleasure of natural running water is praised as the constant motion renders it wholesome and very pure. Stagnant water is the most disagreeable of all; it grows dirty green and gets covered with moss and filth. But of greater interest are the descriptions of the various ingenious and varied devices for displaying these movements of water in cascades. Such as buffets, masks, bubblings, mushrooms, sheafs, spouts, surges, candlesticks, grills, tapers, crosses and vaulted arches.

Unfortunately, by the time the distinguished subscribers to this book had received their copies, they might have read Joseph Addison's *Remarks on Several Parts of Italy in the Years 1701, 1702, and 1703*. He says little about water in the gardens, but does mention that the French obtained from that country all their ideas about waterworks but excelle in them not because they had better tast but from their greater riches. That boo was published in 1705 and was one of th first broadsides in the famous attack o formality in garden design launched b Addison and Pope which led towards th creation of the English landscape garde style.

In about 1718 one of England's mos delightful 'waterworks' was begun b John Aislabie at Studley Royal in York shire. Called 'the long canal' it of cours has a distinct formality, but lying as i does in a steep valley seems to have distinctly different quality from anythin in James' book—though Aislabie was subscriber to it. When his son acquire the abbey itself, his extended waterwork showed a quite different, gently curvin water plan. But th whole, combined desig produces what one ca now only call a com plete spiritual—or per haps aesthetic—qualit remote from all that i described by James.

It shows in on illustration, as it were the elements of the use of sheets of water as feature of garden desig quite distinct from th formal Continenta manner and moving t the English landscape style. Perhaps the finest example of this can be seen at the Nationa Trust's Stourhead property in Wiltshire—provided one looks at it carefully with a most acute hindsight. The scene was created in its original and purest form by Henry Hoare between about 1740 and 1750. It was a valley in which emerged the springs that are the source of the River Stour. They supplied the water which filled the irregularly shaped lake that Hoare formed within the contours of the valley and on whose banks with their bays and promontories he placed the ornamental buildings that are still there, mostly of classical origins and allusions and designed by the distinguished architect Henry Flitcroft, forming possibly the greatest waterscape in England. But to see it as such, as its creator intended, you must make a great effort of imagination. You must obliterate the rich and varied collection of ornamental trees, most skilfully chosen and placed, that now spread around the banks. You must see the sides of the valley, now richly wooded, bearing high up only beech and fir. This famous planting did not begin until 1791, after Henry Hoare's death. Prior to that, the scene was simply a design in water only, decorated merely by superb buildings to display the knowledge of the widely travelled, scholarly owner and his friends and admirers.

Another more or less contemporaneous waterscape, this time dependant on mechanics, was formed in Surrey at Painshill by the Honourable Charles Hamilton. Here he enlarged the River Mole, using an ingenious pump of his own invention. However, the water was only part of the landscape, if a major one.

Stowe in Buckinghamshire seen today is the consequence of a slow development employing many hands whose ornamental water has developed from a regular, octagonal pool designed by Charles Bridgeman, an early pioneer of the informal, to its present free style.

Even before Hoare and Hamilton had set out to work, William Kent (who worked at Stowe) the protégé of the great Earl of Burlington, had demonstrated the irregular use of water in the garden at Rousham in Oxfordshire which he 'improved' in a quite original manner. The remains of the old formal garden still lie beside the house above the Cherwell. But Kent's newer part is on an irregular, and in places quite steep, slope dropping down to the river, which is not straight and canal-like but takes the form of a sharply-angled, irregular Z. This is reflected throughout the plan.

All the talents of the new garden movement from Bridgeman onward and including Kent designed at Stowe, making it a patchwork of styles. Working then as a gardener, at first in the kitchen garden, was the incipient creator of the typical English lake, always as part of his designs for the garden as a whole. He was Lancelot ('Capability') Brown. There is apparently no evidence that while there he ever produced designs himself for the place, but all the time he was working under or with the creator of the new landscape style. At his death in 1783 he is believed to have landscaped 170 estates. Many more in his style can be attributed to his assistants, imitators and successor Humphrey Repton. In nearly every one was a lake of a surprisingly natural if eventually rather stereotyped manner, almost always created with an uncanny instinct from a relatively trivial stream We can still see his greatest achievement at Blenheim. Van-

Fountain: wonderful watery whispering madrigal in air,
Rising roulade and fa-la-la falling;
Fountain: shape of a sound, of a limpidly lilting lull to care,
Still as a stone but burbling and brawling;
Fountain: neutral and nerveless and null, in a weeping far from woes,
Lisping in lovely alliteration
Meaning nothing but singing in silence, or dance where stillness flows,
Legato but lively, endless libation
Poured to graceful and shadowy names —Arethusa, Muses, Pan,
Charming by water lest dry hearts harden:
Fountain: solace and sister-glissando to music mute in man,
How did it come to dance in my garden?
P.J.

brugh's masterpiece stands above a considerable if originally undistinguished valley through which flows the insignificant River Glyme. It was crossed, and the castle reached, by Vanbrugh's triumphant viaduct, an incongruity to span such a trickle. Today, it crosses and almost floats above Brown's huge lake which lies between wooded banks and whose source and termination are not disclosed.

The eighteenth century towards its end had almost entirely obliterated the carefully and geometrically contrived waterworks and replaced them with the so-called natural lakes. We can see substantial relics at Chatsworth and a complete, modest example lately restored by the National Trust at Westbury-on-Severn in Gloucestershire, Melbourne Hall in Derbyshire and Bramham in Yorkshire. Little else remains.

In 1770 Thomas Whately published the first of several editions of his *Observations*

on Modern Gardening. So different is it from James' book of the beginning of the century in all the principles and details that it lays down, that one can scarcely believe that it covers the same subjects. In considering gardening, he thought that ground and woodland first presented themselves in importance, with water coming third. It was, he wrote, the most interesting object in a landscape:

... it cheers the dreariness of a waste, and enriches the most crowded view: in form, in style, and in extent, may be made equal to the greatest compositions, or adapted to the least: it may appear in a calm expanse to sooth the tranquillity of a peaceful scene; or hurrying along a devious course, may add splendour to a gray, and extravagance to a romantic situation . . . a deep stagnated pool, dank and dark with shades which it dimly reflects, befits the seat of melancholy; . . . a river is like a hollow eye which deadens the countenance . . . a brisker current which wantons in little eddies over a bright sandy bottom, or babbles amongst pebbles, spreads cheerfulness all around. . . .

Whately went on to analyse all the features, from bridges (utilitarian, planks and old stones, ruined with arches missing) connected with his beloved water, down to fishes and even get so far as to include water birds. The appropriate woodland surroundings also received attention, but of James' basins, bouillons, rigoles, mushrooms, chandeliers and cascades of water, adorned with figures made from marble, brass or lead-gilt, there is no mention.

What may be called the Brownian natural style of artificial waters—entirely English in origin and indeed skilful execution—became a native tradition which continues to this day in thousands of artificial ponds (lined with plastic) in our more expensive suburbia and indeed in the numerous recreational areas that are today created by local authorities.

Finally, there are the great reservoirs in the rugged, rainy parts of our islands which supply our urban areas. Surely Mr Whately would have approved of that great sheet of water penned in between the steep, forested mountains at Llyn Vrnwy which supplies Liverpool, or the chain of lakes in the Elan Valley which water Birmingham. To discuss them would have needed another chapter in his book.
Miles Hadfield

COUNTRY TOWN

Eall know about villages; but small country towns are comparatively unsung, and certainly uncelebrated as a class. Yet the country town reflects local characteristics as accurately as the village; and if it has not suffered too much from the attacks of the last half-century it is as interesting in its own right.

Bungay, a typical East Anglian market town, has kept its character more than most. The market has been reduced to a few Thursday stalls round the Butter Cross; yet the town centre is essentially as it was before the modern changes: that is, its genealogy still shows in its face and outline. And though it has few of the half-timbered houses of the region (a disastrous fire in 1688 swept most of them away), one or two are still left, hidden behind Georgian fronts. The parish church, moreover, with its spectacular tower and the ruins of the priory, as well as the remains of the twelfth-century castle, combine to show the town's real age.

But the four-hundred acre common, just outside the site of the medieval ditch, is probably the oldest monument it has. Reminders of the common's place in the old town's economy are to be seen behind

or alongside some of the houses: small stables or byres to house the cattle and horses fed on the common. Up to 1914 there were numerous small cow-keepers living near it, each owning *commonages*—rights to depasture so many head of beasts. They brought their beasts home through the streets exactly as they did in very early times when safety demanded that they were kept on the right side of the town's defence-ditch. One of the older inhabitants, referring to about 1910, recalled the old practice: 'When you got down to Netergate Street there—dear! oh dear!—you could slide from one end o' thet lane to the other on the owd cows' mess!' The River Waveney sweeps round the common in a huge loop; and occasionally—as it did in 1968—it overflows its banks, more or less cuts the town off, and restores it to the ancient form of the island its name suggests.

Even small communities can absorb alien influences, given time; and Bungay, exposed as it has always been to invaders coming up river from the east, has had plenty of practice. It shows in one of its main streets how it can also 'take in' and blend the gentler influences: Dutch, neo-classical, Victorian, and even early American. A visitor coming in from the west will notice an example of this last influence: a questing eagle perched on a sign-post, an

informative piece of eccentricity; for the eagle was salvaged from a nineteenth-century hand printing press, a Columbian imported from the USA and is a reminder of the town's long history of printing.

The Butter Cross is an excellent example of functionalism married to a decorative symbolism. This structure, robustly constructed with huge timbers supporting the handsome figure of Justice (made of lead) was primarily an elegant shelter for those who came to sell and buy produce. But underneath it there was once a 'sot's hole', to a depth of six or seven feet in the ground. The occasional boisterous townsman, or the dusty-footed traveller who became clamant after his arrival, was brought here to Justice and lowered into the cell to cool off.

Bungay looks out north over the Waveney to the county of Norfolk where being different has been elevated into a principle—so much so that the University of East Anglia at Norwich has recently adopted *Do Different* as its motto. But country towns like Bungay need no such direct affirmation. As long as they are able to ward off insensitive and arbitrary change (which Bungay is likely to do now that it is being by-passed by a road along the site of the old railway) they will continue to be individual and different merely by being themselves.

George Ewart Evans

THE VILLAGE FÊTE

TENT-hiring-out for village fêtes must be a calm, happy, unneurotic life. All you would need would be this great quiet shed, full of huge folds of canvas. Some for imposing green or cream marquees with stout poles with spikes and flags, almost on a circus scale; some in many-coloured stripes, with scalloped awnings, like the tents at medieval tournaments (Stewards Only, perhaps or Judges); simple ex-Army ridge-pole tents (First Aid); medium tents *just* large enough to be called marquees (Teas).

You would only need a lorry and a small work-force, perhaps of two men in their late fifties ('Jack's been with us for twenty-eight years') and an amiable young man, strong as an ox, uncorrupted by urban greed, already a great grower of peas, tomatoes, raspberries and marrows in his own garden. Winter would be spent mostly in quiet maintenance work and drinking cups of tea, and, of course, answering the enquiries from the kind of people who will still be engrossed in the details of this year's fête when a thin piercing note, growing intolerably louder, heard by all but them, comes from over the eastern mountains: the Last Trump.

Of course, this is pure supposition, for all I know the tent hire business is a savage competition where the weakest go to the wall and threatening messages are found pinned to desks with daggers. But really anything connected with village fêtes is on the side of life. In the age of social fragmentation and Sunday supplement features about loneliness, the village fête is still a genuine community event, unselfconscious and happy. And perhaps one could risk a generalization and say the smaller the village the truer this is.

Your basic village fête is very often combined with a flower show, with a Schedule of Entries often filling several duplicated sheets. This will be necessary because there may be a couple of hundred classes, which will include not only *Dahlias; Vase of 6 pompom or ball;* or *Rose; suitable for a Buttonhole in a Vase,* or *Collection of Fruit; six kinds on a tray not to exceed 2 ft. square*—themselves subdivided between entrants who employ gardeners and those who don't; there will also be *Mixed arrangement of flowers and foliage depicting Britain's entry into the Common Market* or *Six Cheese Straws* or *One bottle of wild fruit wine* or, for children under eleven, *Creature or animal made from tinfoil only* or *Largest Collection of Grasses.* Sometimes there will be endearing misprints, like *Cheery Cake* or *Longest Runner Bear.* Entry fees will be

fourpence or fivepence for each class, and a first prize can be all of twenty pence. In other words, it's done for love.

Early in the morning of the fête, or sometimes even overnight, the exhibits will arrive, and all through the morning mysterious men in cardigans from two or three villages away will be working away at the judging. By the time the public arrive in the afternoon this will all have been done; sometimes, in the case of flower arrangement or just the quality of the flower, by standards of technicality beyond the beholder ('gosh, we should have gone in for it, our dahlias are better than that—and look at those lovely ones of Miss Thomas, didn't even get third prize!'); sometimes the superiority will be blindingly obvious ('how on earth does Stan Wilkins get tomatoes like that? And just look at those turnips. They'll have to handicap him next year')

After all these murmurings in the green canvassy twilight of the main marquee we emerge, if this is one of the lucky years, into sunshine that at first has a reddish tinge until our eyes are adjusted. Flower show or no flower show, the fête will almost certainly have someone to Open it, although this function often takes place at 3 p.m., long after the main battles in the second-hand stalls have been fought (and you really *can* get bargains; my perfectly-good copy of the complete poems of Wordsworth cost threepence, predecimal, at a village fête). Very often the Opener is a local television announcer or minor character from some serial, but whoever he or she is it can be an unnerving experience, standing on a platform in the middle of a field, saying kind words about whatever cause, if any, the fête is in aid of, making jokes, while all the time various peripheral activities are going on from which not everyone is going to be lured.

These days there will also be a public address system which hardly ever stops; in between tremendous crackling noises, screeching feedback, and pop or martial music played much too loud, it exhorts people to buy tickets for the draw, which will take place after the dancing display by the children, or the tug-of-war, or the trampoline display, or whatever local talent has been laid on. It is very nice to be at the kind of fête where this stops sometimes and we hear instead a little silver band pooming gently away under the trees.

When it comes to sideshows, the eye of man hath not seen, nor hath his heart conceived their infinite richness, from rolling pennies on to numbered squares and throwing little wooden hoops over goldfish bowls or throwing darts or backing mice in a Mouse Derby (the runners

one above the other, on shelves in a glass-fronted case) or bowling for a pig, to the semi-professional attractions; the hand-operated roundabout, the tiny railway in which a real steam locomotive a few inches high pulls children on a kind of wheeled saddle over fifty yards of raised line.

The Trade Descriptions Act doesn't apply, and you can no more be sure of getting a firework display and an ox-roasting at a Gala Fête than at an ordinary one. There is a fair chance that you will find a few ladies in Victorian dress at an Old Tyme Fayre, but even this is not guaranteed.

In fact, the very name 'Old Tyme Fayre' is a kind of indicator that lots of fêtes are springing up where none were at all (making tent hire this cosy growth industry, as I doubt not). Other fêtes are rooted in the past, there's not much point in going or even pretending to know about them if you haven't been around for about three hundred years. In Suffolk the feast given by the farmer to his men and their families after the harvest used to be known as a 'horkey'. A friend of mine, anxious to display his knowledge of this word, said to a farmer one September 'I suppose you'll be having a horkey soon'. The farmer eyed him coldly. 'Up here', he said, 'we call that a *froluc*'.

Some village fêtes develop into specialities that rival county shows in the crowds they attract; steam and vintage cars are a tremendous draw, as anyone knows who drives anywhere near Long Melford (glorious Perpendicular church outstanding even for Suffolk) on the day they are having their Monster Old-Tyme Rallye (*sic*). You can't move for highlie polysshed steame threshynge machines, both vyntage and veteran, converging by every roade upon the Pleasaunce grounde, eke shepherded by ye mobile confitables with ye walkie-talkyes.

Memory seems to blot out wet fêtes. The English summer being what it is, there must be plenty of them ('Rain Fails to Damp Carnival Spirit' it says in the weekly newspaper that comes out the following Thursday). The abiding memory is of piled-up but satisfactorily distant July cumulus, sunshine, cardboard plates and cups, hot dogs, ice cream, cups of tea, trampled grass, canvassy twilight, more tea (not beer, really; there's a great difference between a fête and a *kermesse*), children, flowers, special constables directing people to emergency car parks, loudspeakers, music, swings, cine-cameras, second-hand books and new cakes on trestle tables, a relaxed *community*. And of course, a bit more in the bank for the tentage contractor.

Paul Jennings

WRITERS' REGIONS

THE GREATEST of all dramatic poets, Shakespeare knew instinctively that to be universal you must first be *local*. It's no good starting with grand abstractions, sitting round a café or in a beer cellar talking about Being and all that. You must have a place, and people and weather, to be able to give

> . . . to airy nothing
> A local habitation and a name.

Even the huge drama of Lear's madness, of the passing away of things, of dreadful change, is paralleled by an actual storm and an actual heath. There's a great thesis waiting to be written with some such title as *The Heath and Its Significance in English Literature*. From the grim northern industrial cities it is never far to curlew-haunted, windblown moors; they are an essential part of the passionate stormy drama of *Wuthering Heights*.

England is rich in authors' countries; the Shakespeare Country, the Hardy Country, the D. H. Lawrence Country next-door to the Arnold Bennett Country, the Blackmore (or more usually *Lorna*

William Wordsworth

R. D. BLACKMORE

Doone) Country; there is no real evidence that Badgery Water and Plover's Barrows are real places but people expect to see the bullet mark where Carver Doone fired at Lorna, being married in Oare Church. Visitors try to find 21B Baker Street, where Sherlock Holmes lived.

Wordsworth, the supreme nature poet has his country in the Lake District.

O Nature! Thou hast fed
My lofty speculations; and in thee,
For this uneasy heart of ours, I find
A never-failing principle of joy
And purest passion.

Dickens has the entire south east, including London. Consider the marvellous beginning of *Bleak House*: 'Fog everywhere. Fog up the river, where it flows among green aits and meadows . . . fog on the Essex marshes, fog on the Kentish heights . . . fog in the eyes and throats of ancient Greenwich pensioners . . .': or of Hardy's *The Return of the Native*: '. . . the face of the heath by its mere complexion added half an hour to evening; it could in like manner retard the dawn . . . every night its Titanic form seemed to await something but it had waited thus, un-

moved, during so many centuries, through the crises of so many things, that it could only be imagined to await one last crisis—the final overthrow.'

It is something we share only with Russian literature (you always know what kind of weather it is in Tolstoy).

Even the urban novels of Arnold Bennett, deep-rooted in the Five Towns of the Potteries, or of H. G. Wells in south London, have some of this local strength. Priestley has it, in *The Good Companions*. Any English writing with real life has it.
Paul Jennings

ARNOLD BENNETT

Thomas Hardy

ALL KINDS OF GARDENS

HERE are two immediate, obvious visual differences that strike the visitor to England. In the country the hedgerows divide the dullest, flattest landscape into interesting patterns; but the moment he comes near human habitation he will see that we are a nation that, given a chance, hates tenements and loves houses, largely because a house has a little front garden (visible from the road) often tended even if now sprayed with mud and dust from lorries, and a back garden (visible from the train), nearly always tended. Some new estates have communal lawns, but your true Englishman wants his own, private garden. The whole world loves the British garden and we can boast that the men and women of this country are almost entirely responsible for its creation.

True, during a period in the seventeenth century in the heyday of Le Nôtre and his masterpiece Versailles, we were influenced by the French. The fine houses were built on slightly elevated land and massive balustrades and magnificent ironwork adorned the terraces. Steps led down to the garden and parterre and central *pièce d'eau* where the fountain played.

From the parterre radiated the paths and avenues in starlike formation while vistas seen through the woodland trees showed a distant sheet of water or a charming temple of Flora.

Then came William Kent, who had no liking for formality or the artificial landscape. Lancelot Brown, more often known as Capability Brown, who followed him, also rejected the foreign designs and together the two men returned our gardens to a more natural pattern.

Later in the eighteenth century, the British landscaper had a slight flirtation with his Italian counterpart and this association was also fashionable with the Victorians.

The Italians introduced us to topiary, admired by some and shunned by others, and also taught us to use carpet bedding: it is strange that the controversial topiary is more seen in this country today than any other, and that we remain intermittently faithful to bedding out geraniums and lobelias.

After some years of lull in garden styles we returned to our own way of doing things but Le Nôtre had made his mark: some of his garden discipline, geometric thinking and taste has rubbed off on us and can be seen at Chatsworth, Stourhead, and perhaps in some pocket handkerchief herb garden in a London courtyard.

Good garden taste is difficult to define and even more difficult to come by. Our taste is less distinguished than the French, and our gardens lack some of their grandeur. However, we have grand gardens, among them Hampton Court, Chatsworth, Longleat, Knowle, Penshurst, Blenheim, Cliveden, Hatfield and Montacute House.

Next in importance come the manor gardens that are so typically English, usually facing south and accessible from the house by broad French windows. The

south and west of England is rich with them. The garden was now to be treated as an extra and friendly living room with the sky as a ceiling, and a path led the visitor through the flower garden and shrubbery and back again by a different route.

The vegetable garden was not included in this round and was to be found tucked away somewhere remote or walled in. The English gardener has never approved the foreign habit of growing his flowers and vegetables together although the modern and adventurous will now on occasion plant a few variegated cabbages or an artichoke or two in his flower border.

Meanwhile, the multitude of small Victorian beds with stiff plantings of begonias, heliotrope, cannas and an occasional plumbago remained on the lawns summer after summer.

The Renaissance ambiance lingered on and our gardens might well have remained subservient to the French and Italian traditions far longer if it had not been for two splendid and strong willed gardeners, William Robinson (1838–1935) and Gertrude Jekyll (1843–1932) whose views had much in common. Together they made it clear that what was right in Italy and France was not necessarily right for England. As far as they were concerned, no artificial planting could compare with the beauty of nature. They had no liking for ornamental statuary and a perfect horror of carpet bedding.

William Robinson's classic book *The English Flower Garden* had a tremendous influence on gardeners. Tired of Victorian restraint they were delighted to plant their roses, clematis and honey suckle in profusion and to let them 'toss' together: and why shouldn't the border plants encroach upon each other? They hid the soil and kept it cool.

Robinson had a passion for the Michaelmas daisy and was devoted to the border carnation and viola, and brought back into fashion a host of flowers banished by Capability Brown. His garden, Gravetye, became the garden of the day.

But Gertrude Jekyll was probably the better gardener of the two; and Munstead, Godalming was an excellent shop window. She began by advising many friends but soon turned professional garden designer. She loved wild and old-fashioned flowers and was as anxious as Robinson to sweep away the 'bedders'.

There has been little change in direction since they died. Their pattern was to last for the best part of a century, and they have made our gardens what they are.

We have fine twentieth-century gardens and only lack of space prevents me from writing about more than two of them. Hidcote Manor Garden, Gloucestershire once privately owned and created by Lawrence Johnston and now in the care of the National Trust must surely come first. The owner started from scratch, and planted differently from any gardener before. The series of small gardens, or, as they are now known, 'rooms', are enclosed by superb hedges of euonymus, copperbeech, box, yew, and others and of course the tapestry hedge of mixed shrubs plays an important part.

My last garden is Sissinghurst Castle, made famous by the late Victoria Sackville-West; a very individual gardener and poet. She was outspoken about plants in her articles in the *Observer* and made or marred the future of many of them: fortunately, she was generally right.

Sissinghurst is a lovely garden. Its very untidiness had something of its owner's charm. She was anxious that the flowers should express themselves and had a particular respect for the self-sown seedling. Stressing the importance of colour

Neil Davenport

relationships, she would carry a flower again and again from one border to another to make sure that the lily or foxglove would agree with the gypsy-rose before she dared plant them cheek by jowl.

Flower arrangement led by the Japanese has prompted many gardeners to grow unusual plants and has given a fillip to gardening that has benefited the nurseries.

Large expensive gardens are no longer on the increase and it is the suburban gardener who is to the fore. It is a pity that the shape of his estate, usually a narrow strip, is boring and monotonous. It can be improved if remodelled on different levels, but this is expensive or very hard work, with the result that many of the suburban gardens remain unadventurous, and would be dull indeed if it were not for the roses. The small house gardeners are rosarians to a man: they worship their roses (bless them), the best of which have been bred by foreigners, Poulsen, Kordes, Meilland or Tantau. Second favourites are the dahlias and their fans have grown in number, followed by the 'lucky Jims' with a greenhouse and their prize collection of chrysanths.

On the villa window sill, just as on the sill of the grimmest street in the East End of London, there will often be a window box. The Englishman never changes, whatever his trade or profession—he loves his flowers and the feel of his fingers in the earth—and many a countryman starved in a town will put his all into his window box, be it nasturtiums, stocks, petunias, lobelia or the faithful geranium. After all this is the most intimate of gardens, as enthralling as a slow-motion picture. The proud possessor can watch a button daisy unfold as he drinks his morning coffee, and close as he smokes a final cigarette.

I bring my curtain down on quite my favourite—the cottage garden—a delicious mixture of plants—maybe an unsymmetrical muddle and a law unto itself but a garden of the greatest beauty at which this country excels. In it are all the flowers we cherish, and there isn't an inch of soil to be seen. Rosemary, lavender and hollyhocks jostle each other while in the very front a drift of violas and pinks run riot. There are few stakes and no labels, we know the plants too well for that. There are posies of this and nosegays of that and the Madonna lily is showing off as it enjoys growing in the cottager's garden.

At the end of the year, there are the Christmas roses—then come the aconites, snowdrops, scillas and crocus. The gold daisies, the coronicums and a forward oriental poppy and lupin will hold the scene until the summer explodes. . . .

I am intimate with this garden. I like to think about it, instead of sheep, before I go to sleep and visit it in my dreams.
Xenia Field

30

ᴹANY POLITICIANS must envy the following of television, radio and even mere writing garden experts. Percy Thrower, son of a head gardener, ex-parks superintendent at Shrewsbury, runner-up Pipeman of the Year; Fred Loads, began life with a 4 a.m.–8 p.m. seven-day week at 3/6d, appears on BBC *Gardeners' Question Time* with Bill Sowerbutts, market gardener and Alan Gemmells (Biology Professor).

BEFORE them there was Fred Streeter, with a lifetime in stately gardens behind him when he met the first of them all (C. H. Middleton, not in the picture); he was pure radio, a calm Sabbath grandfatherly, loamy, reassuring voice (great gardeners, like great conductors, must be old). Harry Wheatcroft is equally famous for growing roses and moustaches. Ladies have green fingers too. Constance Spry, Britain's answer to Japan, first told us flower-arranging was an art. Victoria Sackville-West, creator of Sissinghurst, is not in this picture either, but Xenia Field, *Daily Mirror* garden lady, inventor of a kind of 3-D fork (and contributor to this book), is.

GROW IT YOURSELF

NY SUMMER Sunday morning it is a pleasant diversion for people coming out of Mass in Shrewsbury Catholic Cathedral, which is on the town walls, to lean over the ramparts and look some thirty feet directly below them on to immaculate, close-packed, well-weeded, watered and hoed allotments; neat furrows of potatoes, beautifully uniform curtains of runner beans, onion setts, lettuces in various stages of development. And a foot-wide, plank-edged long strip containing the kind of herbaceous-border 'riot of colour' usually only seen on seed catalogues.

These allotments actually belong to the town's bowling club, whose smooth and elegant greens begin at the foot of the drop, and they are let out to their skilled cultivators for an annual rent of five pounds. They are therefore 'non-statutory'; but Shrewsbury, like any other local authority, also has allotments of its own, which must be provided for their rate-payers. In the whole country there are some twenty-eight thousand acres so provided, and about 15½ thousand non-statutory acres; quite a lot of land, in fact, given to this do-it-yourself mini-market-gardening (but it's illegal to sell produce; it is supposed to be for a man's own family). In Ipswich, and indeed most towns, the ideal size is regarded as ten rods (or 1/16 of an acre)—rent one pound a year; Ipswich has 2,393 statutory and 543 non-statutory allotments.

No doubt in these days there is a renewed, *merely* economic interest in allotments. Theoretically, it costs no more to put the thousands of lettuce seeds from a packet into a trench, and plant them out at the two-leaf stage, than it did fifty years ago. Theoretically since you could no more buy the penny lettuce of fifty years ago than fly, the world is full of extremely rich greengrocers. In fact greengrocers don't seem relatively richer than the rest of us. Theoretically, since we still only grow two-thirds of the maximum possible amount of temperate-climate foods in this country, *all* those derelict-looking triangular pieces of land seen from railway embankments should be cultivated with a Chinese-peasant intensity. In fact it doesn't work like that. You have to be a certain kind of methodical, well-organized, soil-loving man to run an allotment; a man, also, who appreciates that there is no taste in the world like that of peas, or beans, that you have picked that very day; above all, a man who enjoys being out there.

It would be nice and simple if allotments were automatically provided near every tower block, in a formal recognition

and encouragement of the urban peasant instinct; in fact the whole thing is more empirical than that. It's the people who like the idea of allotments who get them, although in a queue the non-possession of a garden already does, or should, help. The basic concept is of Static (i.e. non-motoring) but Active (i.e. digging, hoeing, raking) Leisure (i.e. deck-chairs) the last gaining in emphasis.

Allotment holders usually belong to a local association which negotiates with the local authority, and very often deals with applications, does the administration, and not infrequently owns as well as leases land. Some 1,725 of these associations are affiliated to the National Allotment and Gardens Society Ltd, which has just changed its name to the National Society of Leisure Gardeners.

Their President, Professor Harry Thorpe, Head of Birmingham University's Geog-

raphy Department, reminded them at their annual conference of the Thorpe Report's accepted recommendation of a minimum of half an acre of leisure garden per thousand population, which wouldn't seem much if they all came on the same day; so, on to ⅗ acre!

Allotments as such were a very British invention, but now the concept is changing the National Association itself belongs to an international body with head-quarters in Luxembourg. On the Contin-ent flat-dwellers have 'chalet gardens' where they sip wine and sit in the sun; they don't go in for cabbage-growing. But in England this concept has been grafted on to the original allotment idea; there is a good example at Westwood Heath, Coventry, which is a community centre as well. Authorities like Birmingham, Coven-try, Cardiff, Bristol and Portsmouth, are well aware of the value of such relief from the concrete jungle, and are sympathetic to the association's fight to preserve allotment land from the ubiquitous specu-lator. After the war, people tired of Dig-ging for Victory and the movement sagged, many allotments fell into disuse; but now many towns have waiting lists—and not only of old-age pensioners, but younger men who have found that Grow it Yourself is an economic as well as a leisure benefit.

Paul Jennings

2 WHEN the English do think hard about work, they are perfectly capable of making things like the Rolls Royce or indeed the Mini. Sometimes we make a world prototype of something, as it might be the tank or the hovercraft or the linear motor, then we seem to get tired of it—and if you go through the industrial conurbations of the north, or the midlands, you will see why. *Industry* we are thinking vaguely, *technology* . . . let's humanize it, if we can. *Some* of us say this, anyway.

WHATEVER HAPPENED TO FANG MANAGERS?

CCUPATIONS in England, for all its industry, have some pretty un-industrial-sounding names. What everyone in this country does is listed in an official government publication with the title *The Classification of Occupations*. All the jobs are given code numbers (mainly to help census officials; instead of writing out something long-winded like Saggar Maker's Bottom Knocker they can now just put 013). In the most recent edition (1970; it costs £2.50), a few of the more extraordinary-sounding have been weeded out. They no longer list Glad Ironer, Mont Loader, Fang Manager, Odd Stamper, Alpine Lad, Sweating House Foreman.

But right from page one you can see there's a variety of which your average Careers Adviser knows nothing.

There is the trade of Ager Man, Hot Airman and Ice-cream Jack. You can spend your whole life in Ashes, passing from Ash Boy to Ash Land to Ash Man.

You can be a Doll, Detonator, Dynamo, Temple, Toy, Treble Hook, Trim, Tube and many other kinds of Assembler. You can be an Amusement, Booster, Bosh, Burner, Wash-off Cock, Creeper, Crusher, Invalid, Jigger, Montejuice, Mortuary,

Pig, Plodder, Sprinkler or Synagogue Attendant; a Bagger-off, Bagger-out or Bagger-up; a Bayman, Beadle, Blacker or Bluer.

Some of the jobs sound simply as if they require brute strength; Bone Crusher, Ding Man, Stallion Leader, Hard Heading Man, Scruff Man, Lump Man, Mule Man, Knacker, Knocker, Knock-out Man. Others seem to require a steady, trained hand; Tea Pot Fluter, Vamp Creaser, Embellisher of Wood, Needle Eyer, Balustrade Fitter, Enrobing Machinist, Toggle Strainer. Others have a pleasantly traditionalist sound; Besom, Wicker Cart Body, Elastic Brace, Breeches, Hassock, Paper Hat, Hip and Valley, Button-hole, Pouffe, Putty, Dandy Roll or Saddletree Maker.

Some sound as if they would take years to learn; Boot and Shoe Artist, Scribbling Engineer, Drott Operator, Possession Man.

Yet others have the air of being fairly easily learnt; Armhole Draper, Flagman, Flanger, Flasher, Decoy Man, Griswold Hand, Creeler; Clicker, Clocker, Clogger, Clown; Liquorice Hand, Dobby Pegger; Smocker, Smoother, Smudger, Snagger, Snipper, Socker, Refooter (Stockings).

Some could be done with practically no training at all; Egg Breaker, Biscuit Emptier, Clay Boy, Sausage Skin Cleaner, Egger and Washer, Tea Masher, Putter-together (Scissors), Second Man on Lorry, Viewer of Bullets—and, if you've hurt your leg, Hobbler to Dock Pilots.

There doesn't seem to be much for women. There may be a Decoy Man but there's no sign of a Decoy Woman. There only seems to be Alley Girl, Back Girl, Brick Factory Girl, Farmer's Wife and Sheet Woman. Still a man's country, basically.

Paul Jennings

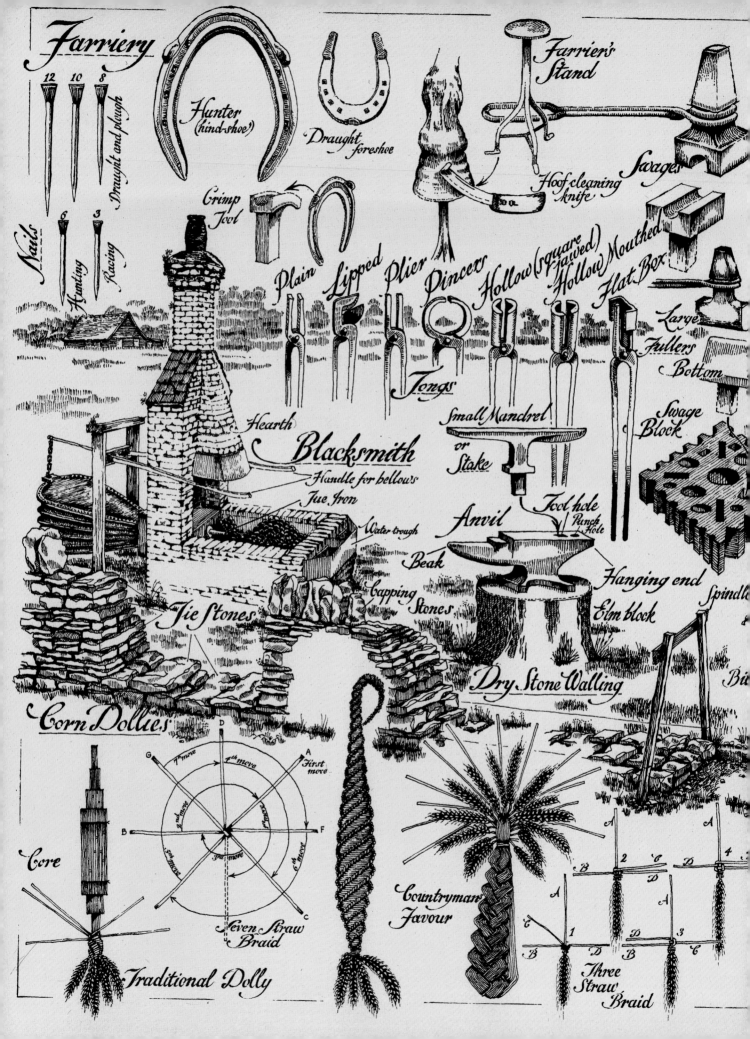

Farriery

Nails
12 10 8 Draught and plough
6 3 Hunting Racing

Hunter (hind-shoe)

Draught foreshoe

Crimp Tool

Plain Lipped

Farrier's Stand

Hoof cleaning knife

Swages

Hollow (square jawed) Hollow Mouthed
Flat Box
Large
Fullers
Bottom

Plier Pincers

Tongs

Swage Block

Small Mandrel or Stake

Blacksmith

Hearth
Handle for bellows
Fire Iron
Water trough

Beak

Capping Stones

Tie Stones

Tool hole
Punch Hole

Anvil

Hanging end
Elm block

Spindle

Dry Stone Walling

Corn Dollies

G D A
7ᵗʰ move 4ᵗʰ move First move
2ⁿᵈ move 6ᵗʰ move
B F
5ᵗʰ move 3ʳᵈ move
C

Core

Seven Straw Braid

Countryman Favour

A A
B 2 C D 4
D A
A A
C 1 D 3
B D B C

Traditional Dolly

Three Straw Braid

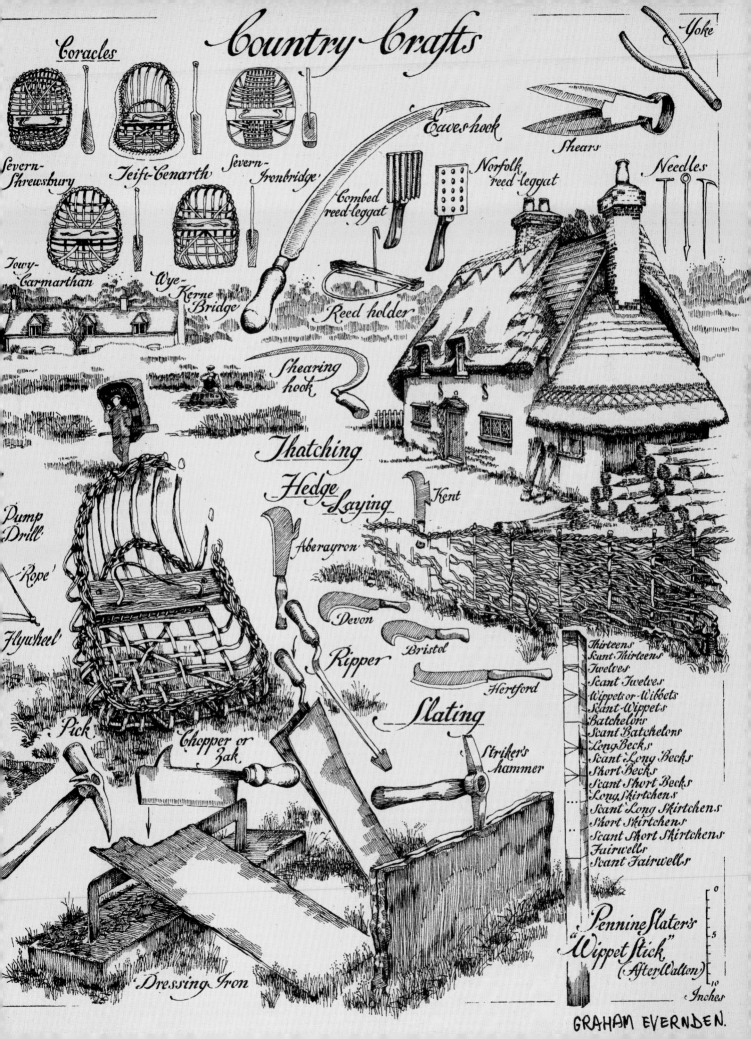

Country Crafts

Coracles

Severn-Shrewsbury

Teift-Cenarth

Severn-Ironbridge

Towy-Carmarthan

Wye-Kerne Bridge

Yoke

Eaves hook

Shears

Needles

Combed reed-leggat

Norfolk reed-leggat

Reed holder

Shearing hook

Thatching

Hedge Laying

Kent

Aberayron

Pump Drill

'Rope'

Flywheel

Pick

Devon

Bristol

Ripper

Hertford

Slating

Striker's hammer

Chopper or Zax

Dressing Iron

Thirteens
Scant Thirteens
Twelves
Scant Twelves
Wippets or Wibbets
Scant-Wippets
Batchelors
Scant Batchelors
Long Becks
Scant Long Becks
Short Becks
Scant Short Becks
Long Skirtchens
Scant Long Skirtchens
Short Skirtchens
Scant Short Skirtchens
Fairwells
Scant Fairwells

Pennine Slater's "Wippet Stick" (After Walton)

0

5

10

Inches

GRAHAM EVERNDEN.

ANYONE FOR YEALMING?

A BOOKLET published by no less a body than UNICEF, the United Nations Children's Fund, called *The Wonderful World of Clothes*, full of saris, and dirndls and other national dresses, shows when it comes to Britain a guardsman (of course), a Highlander (of course), and (a drawing, not a photograph) of an apple-cheeked old woman with a sixteenth-century-looking bonnet. 'In some country districts', it says, 'women still wear an elaborate sunbonnet. *The bonnet has a stiff visor and a frill for protection from the sun.*' (Our italics.)

What country districts? But of course the reason why lots of people in New York (where this booklet was printed) would be quite prepared to believe in these mythical sunbonnets is that they go so well with thatched cottages, which certainly do exist. Suffolk has the highest proportion of them, and in eastern England generally they use Norfolk reed, although you can do it with wheat straw. A foot-thick roof of Norfolk reed will last a hundred years; one of Devon reed, at the opposite end of the country (and the next most thatched) will last fifty.

There are fewer thatchers now, but they are fully employed, and the art and its tools have changed little. The straw is *yealmed* or *yolmed* into straight bundles eighteen inches wide and five inches thick. The horizontal spars which are pinned down to hold it in place on the roof (which has to be steep-pitched) are expertly cut from selected, indeed specially grown, hazel rods with a wicked looking knife held in the right hand cutting down towards the left hand holding the rod. There are few thatchers without a few scars got during their apprenticeship. The *leggat* is a block to beat the thatch into position. And after a lot of cunning work with the bow, the jack and the rake and other tools basically unchanged for centuries, you have a roof often neatly scalloped and sculptured in eastern districts, whereas the Hansel-and-Gretel type upper window with thatch moulded roughly round it is found more in the west of England.

A modern farm worker is often more likely to know about fuel injection or the hydraulics of a ditch-digging machine than to be expert in the rural art of hedging-and-ditching, which has contributed perhaps more than any other to the making of the characteristic English landscape, giving variety and subdivision to the whole countryside (but now we are losing five thousand miles of hedge a year as small fields are joined to make mechanical working easier).

A real stiff hedge is started with stakes, between which the thorns are laid (low, say old countrymen, to check sap rise to the top twigs—hedges should be thicker at the bottom—although scientists say it isn't true about the sap); then as the hedge develops you have living stakes in the bits you leave vertical after splitting.

Paradoxically it seems to be in the eastern counties, flat and windswept, where hedges are most useful as windbreaks, that they are disappearing most quickly. But hedging-and-ditching is no longer automatically a task set by the farmer to his numerous men to keep them busy in winter, and many hedges not grubbed up have been allowed to run wild. (Recent research has proved that you can date a hedge by counting the number of major species such as oak, ash, holly, spindle, maple—self-sown into it. It is one per century. You find a hedge with six species in it, then check the old records where they exist, and it will turn out to be six centuries old.) All the same it will be a long time before the barbed wire takes over completely.

There is nothing like machinery for killing the spirit; you can't imagine fertility rites in, say, the BMC factory at Longbridge. Yet farming, for all its mechanization, is connected to mysterious earth-traditions thousands of years old; the crafts and customs die hard. In some cases the craftsmen go on to turn their traditional skills into modern channels. There are still many thriving blacksmiths. There is one in my own village, and of course they still *do* shoe horses, although these are no longer great Suffolk Punches but lots of ponies which all belong to girls of eleven called Jill. The fire is heated by an electric blower. But the smithy is lined with all kinds of rods and sheets of iron, there are always pieces of farm equipment and suburban lawn-mowers waiting to be repaired, and there is usually a wrought-iron lamp bracket or gate being made as well.

Plato says that the four first, basic people required in a community are the husbandman, the builder, the clothier and (oddly, for a warm country like Greece!) the shoemaker; the smith comes in the next most essential group (since after all, 'the husbandman cannot make his own mattock'). In fact smiths, with their ancient lineage back to Tubal-Cain of Genesis, are as useful now as they ever were. Who in a town, owning a convertible car on which it is fearfully difficult to close the hood (because the lug won't quite reach to the socket it has to fit into, the hood having shrunk) could go as I did to a village blacksmith and have specially made for him the only tool in the world, a kind of magic hooked lever, that will do it for him?

The old sharp distinction between urban and rural people is blurred, and modern mobility has brought an influx of people whose feeling for the earth is perfectly genuine, and only sneered at by people totally corrupted by the machine age. Anyone planting mustard-and-cress in a town garden, like Mr Pooter in *The Diary of a Nobody* has some residual sense of the miracle of the earth.

So it's not in the least surprising that people who are not themselves farm labourers should revivify some of the traditional crafts. As Mrs M. Lambeth, one of the country's experts on corn dollies, rightly observes, 'the art which men no longer have time for has become the new craft of the country woman'.

The very phrase 'corn dolly'—or even the more expressive Northumberland 'kern babby' has a sound of primitive magic about it, a hint of not-far-off days when in some counties the last corn to be cut was trampled down, all the labourers throwing their sickles down together so that the evil spirit lurking in the last corn should not know who had done it. Or elsewhere they thought the corn dolly kept the mysterious spirit of the corn alive till next year. Whichever way you look at it, corn, indeed all growth, *is* ultimately magic.

The basic corn dolly is oval shaped, roughly eighteen inches long, built round a core of straight straws, obviously with more short ones in the middle. Your plaiting straws form a square cross-section (i.e. looking end on) but there are two straws at one corner (i.e. although it's a square there are five, not four), and as you plait this double straw, being thicker, has the effect of an eccentric, so that a spiral ridge grows round the core. ('A very good beginner's straw is Flamingo,' says Mrs Lambeth; 'some others, hollow and easy to plait, are Victor II, Elite Du Peuple, Welcome and Masterpiece.' The WIs know a lot about this too.)

But that's only the beginning. There's the Cambridgeshire Umbrella (looks just like an umbrella, handle and all), the Norfolk Lantern, the Lincolnshire Fly-catcher (they look like chandeliers), the Vale of Pickering Chalice, the Ivy Girl of Kent (very mysterious, like a primitive queen), the Man in Armour, the Mare (from Herefordshire, Hertfordshire and Shropshire; first gang to finish harvesting would tie the last sheaves into the rough shape of a mare—sheaves for head and tail—crying 'Mare!' to slower finishers to remind them wild horses would soon be after their crops); and of course, the Cornucopia, the Horn of Plenty. Which, after all, is what it's all about.

Paul Jennings

UNITE IN LOVE

No, not the battle cry of Gay Liberation, but the motto inscribed on one of the earliest of British trade union banners, that of the United Tin Plate Workers Society. Formed in 1821 by autonomous unions from Liverpool, London and Glasgow, who joined together to 'save the trade', the new union purloined the motto, (directly translated from the Latin), from the medieval craft guild of the Worshipful Company of Tin Plate Workers, alias wireworkers. Being British, with a sense of history as well as purpose, they took not only the motto, but the armorial bearings of the ancient guild for the embellishment of their new banner.

To identify themselves as they struggled to legality, the unions turned naturally to the symbols and insignia of their crafts, including the familiar arms of the guilds. These ancient guilds, once the alliance of masters and journeymen, combined together for the mutual protection of the trade and the common good of their members, were disintegrating under the impact of industrial capitalism. The small workshops where masters worked at the bench alongside their men, were giving way to machine production and specialization. The interests of journeymen and masters diverged and the guilds deteriorated into cliques of middle-class capitalists.

The journeymen, as they formed their own trade societies and clubs, saw themselves as the heirs to the traditions of the crafts of which they were so proud, and had little compunction in adapting the guild arms for their own purposes. In Edinburgh, in 1832, the Society of Tailors, casting an eye on the blazon of the Worshipful Company of Needlemakers, painted their banner with the near naked figures of Adam and Eve and blandly explained that these were the first people wearing the first suit of clothes—fig leaves! The Co-operative Smiths of Newcastle created a powerful banner, 'A voice from the forge', by lifting half a motto, 'All arts do stand' and half a coat of arms, a raised arm with a hammer, from the Worshipful Company of Smiths, 'By hammer and hand all arts do stand'. Plasterers, paviors, masons, brushmakers and weavers, eagerly appropriated the arms of their masters.

The Shoemakers of Nantwich, in 1834, extravagantly engaged the local herald painter, one Thomas Jones, at a cost of twenty-five pounds, to 'Paint for us a banner emblematical of our trade'. He gave them St Crispin, the patron saint of shoemakers, together with the motto, 'May the manufactures of the sons of St Crispin be trod upon by the whole world'. Enthu-siastically adopted by shoemaking trade unionists for generations to come, the device of St Crispin caused a near riot when carried in a trade-union demonstration in Belfast in 1893. The Orangemen mistook the long-bearded St Crispin for their arch-enemy and stoned the banner bearers from the city with cries of 'To hell with the Pope'.

The need to reassure masters and men alike that they meant no revolution was vital at a time when edgy politicians equated dissent with sedition and frightened magistrates were likely to answer demands for reform with cutlass and cavalry as they did at Peterloo. 'Defence not defiance' was the watchword emblazoned beneath spurious coats of arms. 'Combined to protect but not to injure' and 'Reason not force', were the clarion calls to the craftsmen of Britain. Those who edged towards the colours were not merely proud of their skills, but jealous, a tradition to linger shamefully into the twentieth century. The hand of brotherhood was not extended to the unskilled, 'Let us support the trade and keep out others that it would invade', was the motto on an early banner of the Operative Stonemasons.

Emerging trade unionism demanded instant establishment and respectability. As late as the 1890s the proletarian aristocrats of the London river, the watermen and lightermen, freemen and trade unionists, were to paint 1540 on the banner of their Greenwich Lodge, complete with guild motto, 'At the commande of owre superiors' and a portrait of Admiral Clapperton Trevelyan Bedford Pim, RN, in full dress uniform.

The demands of ancient and worthy lineage must have tested the historic knowledge and Biblical scholarship of these early trade unionists. The old United Kingdom Society of Coachmakers took the appropriate guild arms for themselves but improved them by adding the Royal Standard. The printers acquired Caxton and Gutenberg for their banners, while the shipwrights usurped Noah and his Ark. The bricklayers assumed the credit for the building of the Tower of Babel, while the stonemasons laid claim to the building of Solomon's Temple. It was left to the Society of Carpenters and Joiners to make the most audacious assumption of ancient dignity, painting their banner with Joseph of Nazareth and claiming him as 'The most distinguished member of the craft on record and the reputed father of our Saviour'.

Beyond the craft unions, the fight to organize was bitter and bloody. In Merthyr Tydfil in 1831, the colliers marched under banners demanding, 'The reign of justice for ever' and were met by the Argyll and Sutherland Highlanders who left them to count their dead. In Dorset, seven men from the little village of Tolpuddle were arraigned before the magistrates for administering a secret oath. The trappings of secrecy (a necessity where the squirearchy ruled) included two masks, two white robes, a large figure of death, a Bible and a Testament. The gentle lay preachers of Dorset were sentenced to be transported for life, leaving the words of their leader, George Loveless, to echo to this day, inscribed on the Dorset County banner of the union, 'We will, we will, we will be free'.

While the colliers of Wales clashed with the Argylls, the miners of Durham were met by dragoons. It was among the miners, shock troops of the industrial revolution and the vanguard of the working class, that banners became more than signs of identity. In fierce struggles against the 'yearly bond', which bound the colliers as slaves to the owners, the lodge banners became a rallying point for the community and a symbol of resistance to oppression. Strikes were ruthlessly smashed, miners and their families evicted from their homes, neither the aged, the sick, the pregnant, nor those lying injured from their work in the pits, being spared the degradation. When they were starving and homeless, the owners would order the workhouses closed to them and forbid local traders to supply them with food. They were starved into submission, banners had to be hidden away against the day when the union could be rebuilt.

Gradually, as the unions grew to strength and national unity, the iconology of the working class billowed into massive heraldry. George Tutill, banner painter extraordinary, came to weave into the culture of a people already rich in Bible and Bunyan, chapel and pub, society and club, the images of the Renaissance, classical Greece, mythology, mutuality and Masonry. Banners became such a size, up to sixteen feet by twelve feet, that they needed six men working in relays to carry them on the shortest of marches. A Cordwainers banner of the 1860s was described as being as large as a mainsail. A seamen's banner was made so large that it could not be carried and had to be suspended across the street from one friendly public house to another.

By 1871, the miners of Durham were to hold the first of their 'big meetings', bringing fear to the middle class of the city who boarded their windows. The banner on the central platform carried the terrifying slogan, 'A fair day's pay for a fair day's work'. The big meeting became an annual event, a gala day of bands, banners, beer and speeches and a barometer of popularity for the speakers elected to address the gathering. National leaders of the labour movement were lionized by having their portraits painted on to the huge silken sails of pageantry. The names of heroes rang as battle honours on the regimental colours of the poor—Keir Hardie, Ben Tillett, Tom Mann and pioneers of mining unionism like Tommy Ramsay, Alexander MacDonald and William Crawford; 'They being dead yet speaketh'.

In later years the heroes were to become Marx and Lenin, as the miners gave voice to the new militancy of the twentieth century. Inspired by the Russian Revolution and the fiery syndicalism of A. J. Cook, they were to blend the whole with the peculiarly British Owenite dream of a socialist commonwealth. Ramsay MacDonald was painted alongside Lenin on the banner of Bewicke Main, while the Hammer and Sickle was next to the Labour Party emblem on the banner of Wardley Lodge.

But revolution was not to come and the miners suffered the long, lone fight of 1926 and ripped MacDonald from their banners in fury, after the betrayal of 1931. They had to wait until 1947 for the millennium, when the new heroes, Bevan and Attlee, Dalton and Cripps, Shinwell and Horner, adorned banners bearing the proud legend, National Coal Board. 'Nationalization, the dawn of a new era', shouted the blood red banners of Risca Lodge. Others illustrated a jubilant miner climbing the stairway of nationalization, the five-day week, family allowances, National Health Service, peace and security, to the sunny future of socialism.

To have seen a Durham miners' gala with the banners in full flow, is to have witnessed a pageant of trade-union history. To have heard the cheering crowd quieten as a banner passed by draped in black crepe, is to know the true price of coal. Despite the past, the banners show no pictures of hatred, no call for revenge, only hope for the future. They lie, for the most part, furled, gathering dust, a silent witness to the courage of our fathers and grandfathers, who fought for justice and a decent life for ordinary working people.

John Gorman

BRASS BANDS: AT WORK AND PLAY

N THE shadow of a 'dark satanic mill' in a grey Yorkshire village, stands a wooden hut, approached by a covered ramp from the main street. From it emanate sounds famous throughout the world. It is the home of the Black Dyke Mills Band—and has been for over one hundred years.

Being English, the Black Dyke Mills Band is all brass—that is, the instruments are made of the alloy brass and either lacquered or silver-plated. There is no difference, apart from looks, between a brass and a silver band. There is a world of difference, however, between a military and a brass band, a difference not always understood by the mass media. The former included wood-wind instruments and orchestral brass, the latter excludes all wood-wind and substitutes cornets and tenor horns for trumpets and french horns.

A true brass ensemble can make some of the most noble and thrilling sounds in the world. Orthodox concert-goers have come to learn this through hearing, perhaps, Gabrieli resounding in a church, or some huge Mahler sonority, or maybe just in Verdi or Berlioz. The time has passed when brass could be looked down on musically (if it ever was).

The full range of brass-band instruments was introduced in the mid-nineteenth century, at a time when workers in mills, factories and collieries were finding life dull and hard. They needed excitement and colour in their lives. They could see and feel this in the regimental military bands, scattered throughout the country and some started to form civilian and wood-wind groups in the early part of the century. But the possibility of an all-brass combination solved a lot of problems. A brass instrument is comparatively easy to play in the initial stages, so that a musical group can quickly be formed—an advantage re-discovered in the last twenty-five years by education authorities.

Not only did workers find the prospect of forming a brass band exciting, but so did the mill and colliery owners. This was one way of keeping the men happy—and perhaps of providing an advertisement for their products.

By the end of the nineteenth century, brass bands had sprung up in towns and villages all over the country, but particularly in the industrial north.

Black Dyke Mills Band was brought into being in 1855 by the woollen manufacturers John Foster & Son Ltd—and John Foster himself was a horn player in that first combination. The band still is sponsored by John Foster & Son Ltd, but

now less than half a dozen band members work for the firm, although John Foster is probably known on a world-wide basis as much for its sponsorship of the band as for its cloth.

An equally famous band, St Hilda

Colliery, made its appearance in 1896 when colliery workers of a South Shields coal-field decided that they too would like to form a brass band. Until the 1930s, when it turned professional and later collapsed, St Hilda Colliery Band set a high standard of amateur brass playing. Amongst other bands which sprang from the collieries were Grimethorpe, Cresswell, Carlton Main, Lofthouse and Thoresby. They, and a host of others, still exist and

are today supported by the Social Welfare Organization of the National Coal Board.

Brass bands continued to sprout from industrial concerns through the nineteenth and twentieth centuries. Manchester CWS appeared at the turn of the century,

Fodens Motor Works in 1908, GUS Footwear (then Munn & Feltons) in 1933 and Fairey Aviation in 1937. Workers of BEA formed their own band in 1972 and so did members of the Suffolk Fire Brigade.

These bands—begun by enthusiastic amateur musicians and continued with the same enthusiastic devotion—are flourishing in this modern age of television and other forms of canned entertainment.

Fewer and fewer bandsmen work for the

ponsoring body, except in the collieries where the Coal Board grant is dependent upon the proportion of bandsmen employees.

Pockets of the close pre-war liaison between the factory and the band still exist. The chairman of the Hammond Sauce Works is a devoted supporter of 'his' band and creates opportunities within the firm for valuable bandsmen. A

its members the band did not 'fold up', but continued as an independent group.

Alongside the development of works brass bands were the hundreds of village and town bands, where the people themselves bought the instruments, uniforms and music. No small achievement then— or indeed now, when a full set of new instruments can cost around five thousand pounds.

prerogative of the north. As an educational activity, it cuts straight across the social classes and now professional workers join with manual workers to form competent, and sometimes even brilliant, musical units.

Parents form committees to support the school band and when the youngsters leave school, if no community band exists, they either resuscitate one which has long since died, or form a youth band. As the age of the members rises, the word 'Youth' is dropped from the title—and a new community band is born. Such was the progression in the London Borough of Redbridge, which began its brass-band work in 1965. All three bands now exist—Redbridge Schools, Redbridge Youth and Redbridge, the latter no longer supported by the education authority, but by its Parents and Supporters Committee and its own earnings.

One of the attractions of the brass band, not only to young people, but to all age groups (there is no generation gap) is the contest. It has been an attraction for over a century and still exerts its magnetic influence.

What more constructive, more exhilarating way is there of using leisure hours, than by striving for perfection on a brass instrument in solitude, then joining a group of twenty-four others and working with enormous concentration on a set musical work and, a few weeks later, performing it at a contest against other like-minded bandsmen (and women) to be judged for merit by an enclosed adjudicator? Perhaps a championship title or a small money prize for the band fund is part of the stimulation.

The excitement and enthusiasm generated at contests throughout the country has to be experienced to be believed. The prestige contests, the Mecca for all band enthusiasts, are the British Open Championship, held at Belle Vue, Manchester each September, (founded in 1853) and the National Brass Band Championships, begun at the Crystal Palace in 1900 and continued in the Royal Albert Hall, London, each October.

It is certainly the contest which has inspired amateur, English brass bands, to strive for perfection throughout the decades, producing a standard which is envied throughout the world.

The highest compliment is imitation, and English-style brass bands are now springing up all over the continent of Europe, New Zealanders and Australians are great enthusiasts, Americans flock to Britain to hear and observe this phenomenon; and the first brass band appeared in Japan in 1972.

So this is the background of the band in the park, in the carnival procession, or record, radio and television—a high standard of music-making provided by the people, for the people.

Violet Brand

director of the Fairey Company was once a trombone player in the Fairey Band and is now the musical director. When the American company Patchogue Plymouth (Amoco) opened a factory in Consett, Co. Durham in the late 1960s it took over a colliery band, which because of the local pit closure had fallen on hard times. But more usual is the fate of Morris Motors Band which was axed when British Leyland took over. Through the enthusiasm of

One strong reason for not only the continuance, but the surge forward of this very English form of music-making, is the interest taken in the post-war years by education authorities. They too have now seen the value of youngsters learning an instrument and being able to play satisfactorily in a group within a very few months.

School brass bands exist all over the country and are certainly no longer the

ON THE COMPANY'S GROUND

IN almost all sports we have witnessed a phenomenal growth; particularly in those once reserved for the middle classes like squash, badminton and golf, and those with elements of adventure such as sailing and ski-ing. Increased time for leisure, greater mobility and greater prosperity account partly for this increase but the basic human need to face change and challenge, allied to the English craze for inventing ways of having fun are important reasons also. Our sport is still, fortunately, primarily for pleasure and this is why Great Britain has sports councils and not, as many countries, fitness councils. But, whatever the country, sport needs facilities.

Originally their provision was left mainly to private individuals and organizations, then local authorities came into the picture and more recently government. We have in 1974 come closer to, but by no means arrived at, a state system such as our brothers have, in many Common Market and EFTA countries. We still spend far less per head of population than most of our neighbours: in expenditure terms we are poor relations. Even the tax on football pools is still not ploughed back into sport despite the fact that since the war countries like Sweden have made use of the British football results for their football pools, the tax from which provides them with some of the best facilities in Europe. But British sport is on the move and the advent of the Sports Council with executive powers has given it impetus. Within a ten-year plan a scheme has been launched to try to meet the present potential deficit of 447 swimming pools, 815 sports centres and 970 golf courses. There are many providers for sport and recreation—public, private and commercial. One such provider is industry.

In the latter part of the nineteenth century a number of industrial clubs were formed by religious organizations and employers who had a social conscience and sense of moral responsibility to their employees. These were few but they were the pioneers in the industrial sports club movement. Pilkington's Recreation Club was launched in 1847 and its first pastime was the typically English game of cricket. The original grounds have since given way to development but evidence of the original site is the Cricketer's Arms in Peter Street, St Helens, where thirsts were quenched and games analysed over a century ago. The club prospered. Three Pilkington Club members played rugby for England in the 1928 Australian tour of Britain.

In the early twentieth century recreation was becoming part of life in industrial firms. Rowntree of York were leaders in the field mainly through their religious connections. To the traditional games like rugby, hockey and tennis, Rowntrees introduced painting, dances, drama and camera clubs.

The Bournville Athletic Club was another pioneer. The company provided its pavilion in celebration of King Edward VII's coronation. The facilities consisted of sixteen cricket pitches, forty-one tennis courts, four bowling greens and two croquet lawns. In winter these were converted into nineteen football pitches, two rugby pitches, four hockey pitches and four netball courts. The pavilion housed thirty-four changing rooms and fourteen shower baths. In the 1920s most of the activities took the form of interdepartmental competitions and employees took great pride in belonging to a top department.

The industrial clubs were fashioned through the growth in industry and after the 1914-18 war clubs sprang up, many associated with religious and welfare organizations, such as Miners' Welfare. In later years, hit by the Depression many companies closed and some of the clubs were never revived. Impetus was not regained until after the 1939-45 war. In the Second World War many servicemen and women found themselves in parts of the world in which they were able to enjoy forms of leisure which in normal circumstances were beyond their reach, like mountaineering, ski-ing, flying, gliding, sailing and surfing. The post-war era saw new horizons. Women from munitions factories could now, as a new work force, expect provision for off-duty comfort and enjoyment. Greater prosperity and the family car rendered the 'annual Company outing' inappropriate and unnecessary.

It soon became obvious, however, that industry could not hope to provide for all the new emerging leisure opportunities. Thus industry which provided the regular working week with its 'time to work and time to play' and the tradition of company sports, also provided a corner-stone of the working man's leisure—the Saturday half day. This one move took sport for the working class into a new era in which industry was destined to become the lesser provider.

The company sports ground amidst smoking chimney-pots or the green, lush grass of the heath is today a familiar feature on the British industrial landscape. Companies like Cadbury, ICI, Dunlop, Plessey and Laing and the major bankers and insurance companies sport some of the finest facilities, albeit for the fortunate minority of the working population. The Shell Indoor Sports Centre, for example, sandwiched between the Houses of Parliament, the Festival Hall and the River Thames, and run by its Lensbury Club, is the finest indoor centre in Central London. It has superb swimming facilities, a sports hall, squash courts, rifle range, theatre and social provision. However, many companies have no facilities of their own and the majority of small companies are just not part of the industrial sporting scene. Those industrial sports clubs there are, estimated at 1,300, are integral to the complex fabric of British sporting tradition. Collectively the range of facilities they provide is extensive. There are seventy different activities promoted. Soccer and cricket easily head the popularity poll with tennis, bowls, table tennis, golf, swimming and badminton popular, but some distance behind. Some minor sports like archery, basketball, judo and tug-of-war make headway, but the delights of canoeing, pot-holing, pony trekking and sub-aqua swimming for example, are virtually unexplored. But there does now exist a real opportunity for extending the new sports and activities which break away entirely from the mould of traditional sports, although a number of secretaries indicate a tendency of club members merely to 'socialize' and so imaginative programmes may well be stifled.

It would be wrong to get the impression that the 'ordinary worker' is the sole recipient of such benevolence. Some northern clubs may exude a 'working man's' atmosphere but many of the finest facilities and programmes are clearly directed towards middle-class tastes. Survey evidence shows that more 'working class' now join company clubs. But vast masses of industrial workers do not in general participate. Think of the massive walk-outs from factory floors and who would dare ask how many see company sports grounds as relevant in their struggle for a fatter wage packet or in free collective bargaining! Ford's rugby teams, for example, hardly represent the rank-and-file worker. Hence the picture is not an easily understood one. No two clubs are alike. Each company has its own history, problems and idiosyncrasies.

There are, however, common elements and trends. Firstly, while company facilities are usually available to families few companies extend use to the general public, in spite of pressure to do so, and clubs usually limit outside membership. Secondly, club organization is now more in the hands of the employees. Thirdly, the financing of the club is mostly a joint responsibility. On one side the company usually owns the facilities and is responsible for, or contributes substantially to, their upkeep. Large industrial clubs employ a sports and social secretary; the company may also contribute for example pound for pound or make an annual block grant or pay off the deficits. From the other side there are employees' subscriptions from wages, sectional fees, fund raising, social activities, bar takings, bingo, fruit machines and in some cases lucrative lotteries, one reported to bring in over twenty thousand pounds annually.

The experts themselves differ. Some think that management is not quite so sure as it was about the place of sport and welfare in industry today, while in the clubs apathy seems to predominate among membership, so that organization and office-holding falls upon the faithful 2 or 3 percent; often too, less than 10 percent of employees use club facilities. With such a low general level of activity, it is the big company, with its greater numbers and resources, which has an obvious advantage in the promotion of a varied and attractive programme, and notwithstanding general trends, many of these companies are now increasing and improving their facilities. 'But the overall picture is not a particularly happy one, and some smaller companies, unable to sustain an acceptable level of interest in their sports facilities, have already washed their hands of the responsibility and sold or used the land for building development.

Wilf Best, chief executive of the Recreation Managers Association, puts forward a different viewpoint. The trend is a swing back. The vastness of the community all-purpose centre is too impersonal. The idea of going to a leisure centre and having to queue up and to drink out of plastic beakers is not appealing. Interest in the private works club is greater than ever before. Club members like to come and go as they please, get a drink without queuing and play for their own football teams. Employees too are now prepared to pay a little more for better facilities.

Industrial recreation today seems to be concerned with at least three aspects—job attraction, social welfare and physical condition. The fourth, the idea of industry providing for leisure, cannot now be supported. Most workers today like to seek their recreation and self-realization outside work. Despite the fact that large organizations employ more people and are better able to provide recreation facilities, it may well be that the whole industrial recreation movement has passed its peak.

Nevertheless, an association has apparently been shown between being an efficient worker and participating more than the average in recreation activities, although it is difficult to say which is the cause and which is effect. In many companies recreation has become a most effective tool in developing better communication between labour and management. In an age of new industrial revolution—pay disputes, anarchy, strife between management and workers—it is claimed that both worker and manager recognize

the place of recreation in the industrial pattern. Such provision is said 'to benefit the industrial world because it breaks down barriers, relieves job monotony, builds friendships, helps cut absenteeism, improves morale, strengthens public relations and improves community relations'.

Watching television is the most consuming pastime away from work. In a national government survey the next most important activity for men generally was gardening followed by physical recreation, and for women crafts and hobbies, mainly knitting. In all the principal industries membership of the company clubs was found to be highest in the New Towns and lowest in Central London. As much as one in four of men in full-time employment in the New Towns said they made use of facilities furnished by employers, compared with only one in ten in London.

A national survey found large differences between industries in the provision of sports and social facilities for employees; the best provision was generally found in the manufacturing industries. The principal reason for the variation was the relative availability of land for use as playing fields and greater modernity of factories in New Towns, where industrial provision appears to make a significant contribution.

Other countries have taken some leads in industrial welfare. In Sweden for example, central government, local authorities and private firms combine to support recreation. In West Germany there are a number of medically controlled health centres for employee 're-conditioning'. Similar centres exist in many countries—for example in Russia and Soviet satellite countries, Switzerland, Austria, Holland and Israel. Industrial management in many European countries, notably Sweden, France, Holland, Belgium and the 'people's democracies' has begun an assault upon the degenerative effects of modern work. Alongside the more traditional forms of sport, carefully timed 'break gymnastics' or work-bench callisthenics have been introduced and this kind of tension-releasing activity has been well received. In the USSR these activities are described as 'production' gymnastics because of the apparent increases in productivity. A Belgian study noted improvements in production of up to 25 percent. In a productivity-conscious Japanese firm, two teams of girls complementarily work a four-hour shift. Each team spends two hours seated at ergonomically-designed benches doing fine, fingertip precision work. After a break for orange juice they are given twenty minutes basketball or gymnastics, followed by one hour of packaging, which is deliberately non-automated in order to provide a certain minimum amount of exercise for the larger muscle groups.

This seriousness when applied to sporting pastimes is unpalatable to the British sense of fun and freedom, but we must be

aware of industrial consequences and there is much to learn from the experience of others. The promotion of industrial recreation is a complex and demanding job. Recreation leadership is essential; sound philosophy and training is needed. Training in recreation management is now academically accepted and courses at the Loughborough University of Technology and the Polytechnic of North London are now established. The Recreation Managers Association has begun to lay the foundations for nation-wide company sports regional development and the Sports Council has listed sport and industry within its scheme of priorities.

Industrial firms and companies provide over 30 percent of all urban sports facilities according to the *Sports Development Bulletin*. If these facilities become widely available they would obviously contribute greatly to community recreation. At the moment there are some impressive examples of the co-operative spirit in joint planning. In Prescott, Lancashire, British Insulated Callender's Cables Ltd provide a site valued at £50,000 for a new swimming-pool complex, estimated to cost £224,000—which was a joint venture between the Prescott Urban District Council and the Whiston Rural District Council. In addition to assisting two neighbouring authorities BICC have just opened a £230,000 project for the eight thousand members of the BICC Athletic and Social Club.

In Ellsmere Port six companies own private grounds of eighty-five acres. All are attractive and well maintained. Yet a survey has shown that less than 10 percent of the employees use these facilities; in one case as little as 5 percent. A partnership was evolved with the major companies in the borough to provide jointly a large sports complex in the town under the aegis of a sports trust.

Companies too are sponsoring sport in the form of scholarships and awards, events and coaching schemes. For example, the Guinness, Walls and Coca-Cola Award Schemes have injected new life into sports.

Does company sport have relevance then today? I believe it does. Industry should accept the idea of co-operation with other community organizations. It should take any opportunity to lessen distance between factory and home. It should encourage the training of recreation managers. In an age of automation industry should view recreation in a work context also, as part of good working conditions. Above all work should be designed to maximize job satisfaction and human enrichment so that the vestige of the Industrial Revolution with its 'time to work and time to refresh for work again' makes way for a new revolution where industry and community welfare are indivisible.

George Torkildsen

TOP OF THE BILL
AT THE MECHANICS' INSTITUTE

SHOCKED—and rightly so—by the dismal life of the working classes, a splendid man of the nineteenth century, the Reverend Henry Solly, resigned from the Unitarian ministry to try and raise three million pounds, no less, for a chain of 'working men's clubs' all over the country in a national club union. (He also edited the first Labour paper, the *Beehive*.) In 1862 the postmaster-general is said to have introduced him to his wife, saying 'This is Henry Solly, my dear, who believes that Heaven consists of working men's clubs'.

But you couldn't drink or smoke in them let alone be entertained by someone like Frankie Howerd or Michael Bentine. So it wasn't long before a new president—admittedly not exactly a working-class figure, since he was Lord Rosebery (but this was 1875) said:

> . . . the working men . . . are not to be patronised, and fostered, and dandled . . . each club should be altogether free from vexatious infantile restrictions on the consumption of intoxicating drinks and all similar matters . . . secondly if they are to be a great success they should be self-supporting. Thirdly, they ought to set their members some object higher than the mere social object of getting a comfortable place in which to meet. At the same time it will be very easy to aim at too much. From time to time one reads of enlightened miners returning from their underground toil to the consumption of aesthetic tea or the discussion of the subtleties of 'Hamlet' or the mysticism of Greek literature.

These are fragmented times in which 'getting a comfortable place in which to meet' or even meeting at all, is not so 'mere' as it might have seemed in 1875. Today the clubs cover a wide spectrum from brown-leather-and-skittles to chromium-neon showbiz; but they are certainly one of Britain's loudest answers to the telly.

Music-hall had long battles with the 'legit' stage for the legal right to do 'drama'; helped by Dickens it won half-hour performances by stars like Tree or Bernhardt, and final respectability in the first Command Performance in 1912. But it began as a place for turns, attached to a pub; and as the theatrical part began to outgrow the pub part, the licence to drink while you were watching was withdrawn.

The new-style clubs (there are a hundred of them outside London) which grew all over the country, largely as a result of the controversial Gaming Act of 1959, have proved a life-saver to the good old music-hall tradition.

In the 'dying' days of the music-hall Jimmy Wheeler (he with the battered hat, the violin, and the invariable finishing line 'Ay, ay that's yer lot') was addressing the audience at the Ipswich Hippodrome. In between references to a recent change-of-sex operation ('ah, a tricky operation that is; one slip of the knife and Bob's yer auntie') and family allowances ('now they're *payin'* yer to stay at home') he asked the audience 'now why do you think I come up here every day, seventy miles up that bloody awful road? *Because I love the music hall*. I came on a stage like this when I was five years old. Oh, I know why you've come 'ere. It's because you've seen me on that bloody goldfish bowl' (he was then in a regular television series). 'Cor, *murder*, that is. One sketch, and it's *gorn*, they want a new one. How do you suppose we can practise? How do you suppose there are going to *be* any more comics if there aren't lots of places like this for 'em to learn? Don't let 'em take the old Ipswich Ippodrome away from yer!'

But they did. And just in time, to supplement the scarce pier-end shows, came these clubs, some of them enormous. (A capacity audience at Batley, Yorkshire is fifteen hundred). They were big enough and rich enough, in fact, to go beyond native-born music-hall talent and attract world names such as Louis Armstrong, Sammy Davis, Sinatra, who might by-pass mere London on their way.

At one time it looked as though the proliferation of gambling-based clubs would go too far; but then in any case the Gaming Act was amended, controls being made stricter. And the net effect was the survival of the better ones.

Charlie Williams, the famous black comedian born in Yorkshire, is a man who like many of the new generation of comics, impersonators, etc., made his name in the clubs. Coming on in his brown-check suit he mops his face. 'My Goad', he says in purest Barnsley, 'it won't come off!' He leers at the audience; 'if thee doan't laugh, Ah'll coom an' live nex' door to thee.' In the original days of music-hall, comedy dealt with problems familiar to the working-class audiences; rent, moonlight flits, mothers-in-law, money, class ('Our Lodger's Such a Nice Young Man') and took the sting out of them in a comfortable, unbuttoned, evening-out atmosphere.

And of course it was Charlie Williams who first told the immortal story of Enoch Powell. Knocker Powell went up to Pearly Gates and knocked, an a voice inside said 'Who dat out dere?' so Knocker said 'forget it!'

Paul Jennings

3 OF COURSE, 'an Englishman's home is his castle' is a political saying, implying that if *we* ever had secret police knocking on the door in the small hours, the householder would slam it in their faces (or so we like to think; we haven't had to try it yet). But it is also a domestic saying. The Englishman's home is his home. For an outdoor people we spend a great deal of time poring over Ideal Home Exhibition catalogues and putting up two kinds of wallpaper in every room, and no small town is without at least one do-it-yourself, shop. We're the people who invented the invitation card on which are printed (or, in the best circles, engraved) in copperplate script simply two words: At Home.

INTERIOR RECOLLECTION

O there's been a lot of change
My son, my daughter;
Why, in this very room
   we had a range
With four green-tiled
   doors and a push-
   pull knob.
We got hot water
From a back boiler, and tea from a kettle
   on the hob;

O, there's been a lot of change.

In fact, if you lived in this house,
My children, all so cherished,
As it was when I was a child, I think you'd
   grouse!
Take that landing, at the top of the stair;
It was brown linoleum, cold and bare,
Your bare feet would have perished,
There wasn't this carpet all over the
   house.

We're not all that old,
Your father and mother
But we took it for granted a child's room
   was cold;
Is it to you, as it is to us, such a *treat*,
The thermostat-click (though not that
   VRROOM), and the constant heat?
It was rather other
When we were kids.
   It was cold.

I suppose there was lots of clutter
In our generation;
A box with a wire gauze door for meat and
   butter,
The kitchen table-top hinged, a patent
   wangle,
You tipped it up, and there on top was a
   mangle,
A rumble of roller-rotation,
Water squeezed through a little zinc
   gutter.

And how much seemed to be brown;
There were brown armchairs
The bannisters too were brown; and for
  half-a-crown
We bought a tin of brown varnish and
  painted the floor
All round the carpet, which ended two feet
  from the door;
Of course, some colour was there
But a lot seemed to be brown.

I remember the kitchen sink
Before there were plays about it,
A great deep china thing; and in a way, I
  think
That buying the double one, all in stainless
  steel,
Was hardly worth the expense; I mean,
  now, I feel
The washing-up machine (I couldn't live
  without it)
Does it much better (I think).

Well, of course, in my young days,
My daughter, my son,
Everything was another shape, and was
  done in different ways,
The wireless (not the radio) had a fretwork
  speaker;
Sometimes I think we're neater,
  sometimes bleaker,
The two rooms knocked into one,
And everything cubic, in various ways.

Well, the twentieth century woke us,
My children, my dear ones,
We got rid of the clutter that threatened
  to choke us;
But where is the centre, the core of the
  house that I'm keeping,
Where is the fire in the hearth, with the
  little flames leaping?
Switch off the telly, my near ones,
I'll tell you the Latin for 'hearth'; it is
  focus.
Paul Jennings

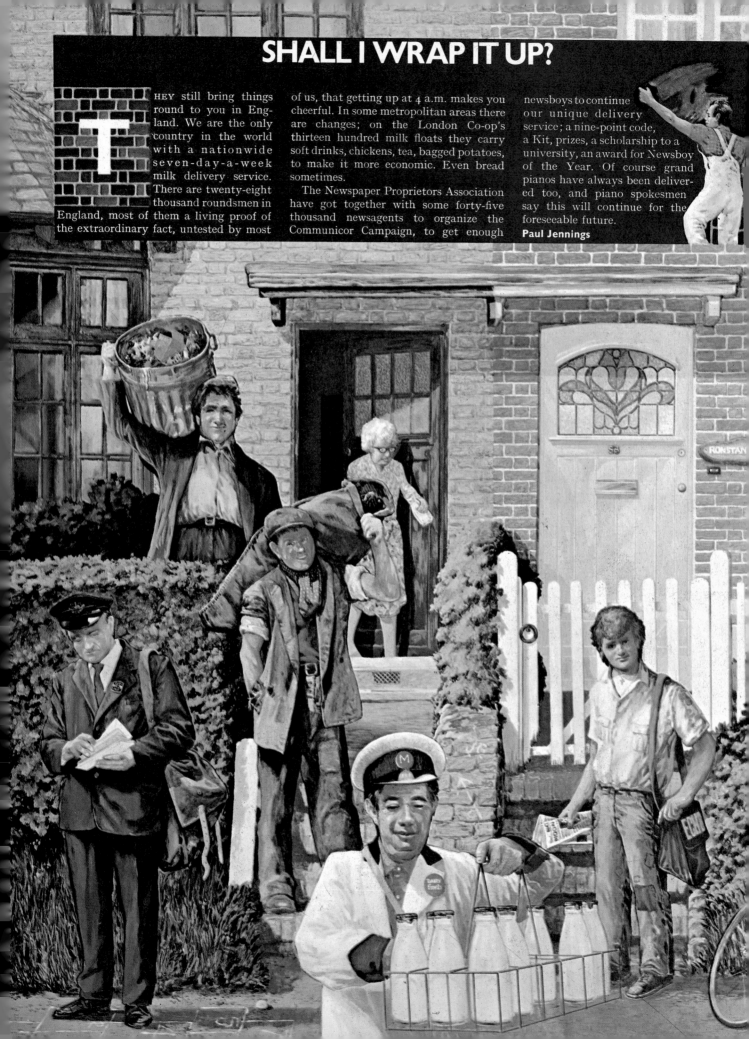

SHALL I WRAP IT UP?

THEY still bring things round to you in England. We are the only country in the world with a nationwide seven-day-a-week milk delivery service. There are twenty-eight thousand roundsmen in England, most of them a living proof of the extraordinary fact, untested by most of us, that getting up at 4 a.m. makes you cheerful. In some metropolitan areas there are changes; on the London Co-op's thirteen hundred milk floats they carry soft drinks, chickens, tea, bagged potatoes, to make it more economic. Even bread sometimes.

The Newspaper Proprietors Association have got together with some forty-five thousand newsagents to organize the Communicor Campaign, to get enough newsboys to continue our unique delivery service; a nine-point code, a Kit, prizes, a scholarship to a university, an award for Newsboy of the Year. Of course grand pianos have always been delivered too, and piano spokesmen say this will continue for the foreseeable future.

Paul Jennings

MEAT AND DRINK TO US

THE RIBS OF BEEF, wrote Thackeray, 'this is the meat I would eat were I going to do battle with any mortal foe. Fancy a hundred thousand Englishmen, after a meal of stalwart beef ribs, encountering a hundred thousand Frenchmen, who had partaken of a trifling collation of soup, turnips, carrots, onions, and Gruyere cheese. Would it be manly to engage at such odds? I say, no'.

Perhaps the roast-beef image (even though it presented the Continent with the word *bifteck*) is no longer what it was, even though in their heart of hearts Englishmen still don't think a meal is a meal unless it has meat in it. And, as a general rule, the farther north you go the more gravy they put on it. But either there are more people and fewer cattle, or people outside this island have more money to offer those who produce our own unequalled beef, or the Common Market means we can't get it from Australia (but what about the Argentine, it used to be all right with *them* and they weren't even in the Empire?) . . . whatever the cause, it's getting a bit difficult to keep up the standard, and people nowadays tend to enter the butcher's shop with little pads so that they can do sums.

In fact it's a great mistake to think that if you can't have roast beef and two veg the only other choice is that still uniquely British thing, fish and chips, and if you can't have that you might as well turn your face to the wall. On the contrary, this richly regional country can produce a wealth of regional recipes which for sheer sprawling Dickensian—nay, Shakespearean—variety makes the Continent, with all that veal (don't their cows ever get to grow up?) look very unadventurous.

Here, at random, are some of the ones sent in to the *Farmers' Weekly*: Old Norfolk Partridge Stew, Granny Morgan's Brawn, Two Dishes From One Fowl, Gipsy Pie, Kromeskies ('a good way of using up herring roes'), Fish Ramekins, Stelk (made with rather old spring onions, potatoes and milk), Somerset Rabbit, Cornish Potato Cake, Quorn Bacon Roll, Huntingdon Fidget Pie, Turkey Pork, Buckinghamshire Dumplings, Oldbury Tarts, Wiltshire Lardy Cakes, Wiltshire Porkies, Dressmaker Tripe, Toad Special, Coventry Godcakes, Water Lilies (made from turnips and cheese), Pineapple Upside-down Pudding, Economy Jam, Emergency Marmalade, and Yorkshire Old Wives' Sod. What a list! We don't want to ban imports, but by jingo, if we do. . . .

It is cruel to print a title like Yorkshire Old Wives' Sod without telling people how to make it, so here, by courtesy of the *Farmers' Weekly*, is the recipe:

> 5 good sized eggs
> 3 gills new milk
> pepper & salt & butter
> 2 thin oatcakes

Break the eggs into a basin and beat for two minutes. Add the milk and seasoning, mixing well. Have ready a baking-pan nicely greased with fresh butter. Pour in the beaten eggs and milk mixture. Next break the oatcakes into pieces about ½ in. square. Sprinkle them on top of the sod. Add a few nuts of butter and place in a moderate oven. Bake for 20 minutes. If oatcakes are lightly toasted and buttered before breaking up they make a tastier dish.

The Somerset Rabbit which adorns this page turns out to be a very simple matter:

> Put alternate layers of grated cheese and chopped onion in a pie-dish, topping with cheese and breadcrumbs. Bake in a medium oven till the onion is cooked.

Most of the recipes involve rather more than that! Cookery, like music, is an art that exists in *time*; and time is what you need either for adventurous dishes encountered by the new post-war holidays-abroad British—*Carbonade Flamande* (but made with Guinness), *Bouillabaisse Ratatouille*, even good old *Spaghetti Bolognese* —or for native spin-the-meat-out hotpots and whatnots. And England is not alone in having more working wives with less cooking time, and therefore more frozen food, more Instant This and Ready-to-serve That, than ever before.

Certainly there is a close connection between regionalism and good cooking, dating from the old days of limited transport and even more limited communication. Nowadays, anyone who takes the trouble to study a book like Robert Carrier's *Great Dishes of the World* and rummage round for the right ingredients can produce a fair approximation to *Maître Paul's Blanquette de Veau Menoigère* or *Délices de Sole Lucas Garton* or something grandly English like Oxford's Magdalen Venison; and it is less true now that if you really want to know about York Ham you must go to some discreetly famous pub tucked away in the moors. They offer you *Jambon de York* in Barcelona these days, although it comes from pigs born a long way from Huddersfield.

On the other hand, it is still true that because of the cows, the grass, the air, the water, the conjunction of the planets and the skill of certain people in and around the village of Godmanchester, Huntingdonshire, that is where the uniquely noble Stilton cheese comes from. Unless you're giving a party for a hundred people you're not likely to have the full 14-lb monster; just a wax-covered potlet.

Devonshire cream teas never quite taste the same outside Devonshire. Holiday-makers send tins of the even clottier Cornish cream to friends back home in Lancashire, where there is Aylesbury Duck as well as Lancashire Hot-pot on the menu. You can buy 'Melton Pork Pies' almost anywhere. . . .

There is more of everything nowadays, good as well as bad, but certainly the undoubted improvement in the kind of meal you could expect to get on a night out, particularly in small towns where before the war there might have been only one caff with steamy windows and net curtains, that closed at 9 p.m., has been at least matched by home cooking with aspirations to the A-level grille.

All the same, that doesn't necessarily mean endless experimentation. There are such things as national dishes. It's not so much that a French cook couldn't make a Steak-and-kidney Pie as good as the one you get in that sand-floored, American-haunted pub off Fleet Street, The Cheshire Cheese—or as in millions of English homes, some more frequently than others; it's just that she wouldn't want to. She would have other virtues, although it would be difficult to think of them while you were actually eating the pie. And the same goes for Boiled-beef-and-carrots, and the Sunday Joint, and Bacon-and-eggs (Lord, how they do fuse them together, in a sort of Bacon Omelette, in Abroad!); and even A Good Cup of Tea.

There's an enchanting Beatrix Potter record in which Mrs Tiggy-winkle (a hedgehog-washerwoman, if you remember) sings, in a delicious compressed hedgehoggy voice:

> When the troubles of the day are over
> There is NOTHING can comfort MEE
> Like a NICE
> HOT
> STRONG
> Cup of TEA

Coffee is making inroads. We have fallen from our peak consumption of 10 lb. a year for every man, woman and child in the country to somewhere round 8½ lb, but we are still undisputed world champion tea-consumers, followed at some distance by Australia, with, oddly, middle-eastern countries like Iraq coming up (and you can see workmen on Turkish building sites drinking not Turkish coffee but, imagine, Turkish tea). *Paris-Match*, in an aggressive interview with Mr Heath, kept going on about *le pause thé* as one of our great weaknesses, saying virtuously that this sort of thing was unknown among French workers. So maybe we're catching up. Just let them wait till we've got it down to, say, only 5 lb. a year per capita; *then* they'll have to look to their surpluses.

Paul Jennings

NOW THERE ARE PLENTY OF TEASPOONS

ASK a silly question, and even in a transport café, which is almost invariably a friendlier, more personal sort of place than just any old public café, and you will get, not a silly answer, but one that without any rudeness makes you see it *was* a silly question.

'Why,' I asked the cheerful bloke in the white coat behind the counter at one of them on the A5, 'is roast beef (or, it said on the menu, roast pork, or ham or sausages) 'with two veg and chips thirty-eight pence, but with mashed potatoes forty-one pence? I should have expected it to be the other way round.'

'Because the oil for making chips costs £9.50 a drum,' he said.

'Well, that ought to make the chips dearer.'

'So they are.' He turned to look at the board, which was one of those black ones with white figures and letters stuck in. (I noticed that the nearest to anything alcoholic you could get was announced as CHANDY.) 'Cor,' he said, 'you're right, I've got 'em the wrong way round. You're the first bloke that's noticed. But of course most of the fellers *know* what it costs, they're regulars, been coming for years.'

Probably the difference between a British lorry driver and a French *routier* is that the Frenchman thinks *first* of the food (and very often drink) whereas the Englishmen, while not scorning these things, thinks first of—well, a certain relaxed matiness, a certain almost club-like quality.

When you come to think of it, the very word café is a misnomer. Once it was indeed exclusively French, everybody knew what was meant by 'café society'. Then it came to mean a place with light-green painted wicker chairs to which ladies in hats in south-coast seaside towns went for their elevenses; and finally, downgraded to 'caff', it came to mean the sleaziest, steamiest—windowed, most leather-jacket-and-thug-haunted place in town.

The transport café is none of these things, and never has been. It is something advertised, in alphabetical order of counties, in the yellow pages of the little red *Transport Driver's Pocket Guide*. Mrs This, George and Ethel That, 'Always a Welcome.' Outside I had been talking to Mr Goode, who has been delivering new lorries and cars and driving commercially for thirty years.

'Funny, really,' he said, 'I know it's the lorries that make a lot of the noise in the modern world; I feel sorry for the poor blighters that live near Spaghetti Junction on the M6. But we like a bit of peace too. Lot of fellers come up the A5 instead of the M1 if their schedules allow it. The other day I was at one of those service stations (I don't think the prices are any lower in the transport part than they are in the civilian part) and I paid twenty-five pence for a sausage sandwich with one sausage in it.' (I shall never think of frankfurters again as anything but sandwich sausages, which is all they are when you come to think of it.) 'I've just been in there, and for twenty-eight pence I had *three* sausages, very good ones, fried egg, baked beans and tea.'

This may not be *Relais Routier* stuff (it's not *Relais Routier* prices, either); but your professional transport café owner knows what his clients want, and he knows that the days have long since gone when they would put up with anything. 'I was in one place, around tea-time,' another driver said, 'and there was a feller asked for some cake, she brought it with her hand all over it, and he *skimmed* it at her, like a quoit, he said you don't think I'm going to eat that *now*, do you?'

There is a spectrum, of course. Some lorry drivers stay at places which would be rather put out if you described them as transport cafés at all. The go-ahead container port of Felixstowe has what can only be described as a very good hotel for its drivers, complete with high-security lorry park, modern restaurant, bar, television, recreation rooms, the lot—and this is by no means a pioneer venture. A firm called Taylorplan, who specialize in industrial catering, not only in static situations but also in, for instance, building sites, run several 'Lodges' (also advertised in the drivers' 'Little Red Book', (Single or Double Rooms, Licensed Bar, Colour Television Lounge, Baths, Showers, Evening Meal if Required, Night Porter, Early Calls Organized . . .) where 50 percent or more of the clients, by no means necessarily drivers at all, are permanent residents—and where bed and breakfast costs £1·70.

In the A5 café, which had green walls and orange curtains, there was a more utilitarian note. Three men called George Riman, George Adams and Reg Lea, who had parked two enormous, long, yellow low-loaders belonging to a midlands machinery firm, were drinking good coffee from cups without saucers. 'You can always tell a good one,' said Mr Riman; 'it's a very simple test, same as for any other restaurant. If it's good, you'll see a lot of lorries parked there—and believe me, when you know what it's like manoeuvering an artic into place when there's a lot there already, you know it's got to be good to attract us.'

'Remember The Dell?' said Mr Adams. 'I had a marvellous steak dinner there. I asked them how they managed it at the price, and they said they believed in big turnover and small profits.'

'*Nobody* believes in small profits,' said Mr Lea.

'You know what I mean,' said Mr Adams, 'a little on each meal, a lot altogether, if there's a lot of meals. But sometimes they get tarted up too much, frighten people away. There was a place on this very road, but a good way from here, and it used to be *awful*; bits of black stuff on the plate, everything slopped about. Then it came under new management, they had check tablecloths, and all that, but they didn't treat you as a *person*.'

'Everybody knows which are the good ones,' said Mr Riman. 'I think there's two things about transport cafés. They're run by the people themselves. And a lot of them, especially the older ones, are run by people that used to be in the Services, and there isn't much you can tell *them* about keeping a place clean. The toilets, that's another good test.'

The one here was spacious, indeed airy, in a Victorian kind of way, and had the air of having just been thoroughly washed out with some kind of no-nonsense disinfectant; it stood between the café and the accommodation (for seventy, men only, singles only). I had a 'Chandy', as the Abelson men started up their enormous vehicles and left. A few minutes later, I passed them on the hellish, howling, three lanes thick last bit of the M1 into London, and we had a cheerful exchange of horn parping before the huge, impersonal city swallowed us up; a place in which it is very difficult indeed to find a place to eat where most of the clientele seem to know each other, and keep coming back.

Obviously lorry drivers aren't the only people on the road, though it may sometimes seem so on the M1. For *non-lorry* drivers good cheap eating has in the past been very hit-or-miss indeed. It is fashionable to complain about any kind of standardization, but it *can* be upwards and therefore a Good Thing. I have no idea if *Which* has done anything on Wimpy Bars, and don't really care; I just know a Wimpy (with onions) is a tasty quick reliable snack. And on dismal erstwhile foodless roads, not motorways but important trunk routes, the motorist may now often find a place called Little Chef, offering fare from hamburgers up to steak (no alcohol) with (surprise surprise!) cheerful attendants at 10.45 p.m. Nearly 200 operating now. It's not unknown for lorries to stop there too, so they *must* be all right.

Paul Jennings

U'D BE SURPRISED

THE whole U and non-U thing in England is reminiscent of what is known in music as Contrary and Conjunct Motion, where you have a scale coming down and, looking like a mirror reflection in the score, one coming up simultaneously to meet it. It isn't a straight line at the top, with all the people at the bottom on an ascending line trying to get up there and sound and look just the same.

On the contrary; the people at the top are trying to come down quite as fast as the others are trying to come up. Not literally, of course, in the sense of giving all their dividends away to the poor; not on your nelly.

It is all very confusing to those who like things neat, the way they are abroad. There is no Continental equivalent, in earlier days of the very ungrand, democratic kind of knight you get in Shakespeare, like Sir John Falstaff or Sir Toby Belch, a lord of the four-ale bar—or, in our own day, of the Honours List. A Comte is a Comte is a Comte, a dapper bloke with a hairline moustache, wearing riding breeches, in a château hidden in about a hundred square miles of beech-woods. You don't catch *him* opening the village fête, or his wife giving coffee to the WI. Above all, there's simply no Continental equivalent of that sublime English combination of opposites, that walking oxymoron, the socialist peer (whether life or not).

It is the middle class, with their passion for order and reason, who have sought to impose some kind of structure on what is in fact an eternally malleable and bubbling class situation (as Chesterton remarked, the public schools are to

educate the fathers of gentlemen), and quite a lot of them have been shamed by the late Miss Mitford into saying lavatory instead of toilet, pudding instead of sweet, and the rest of it. Paul Dehn, in a brilliantly funny article, once pointed out that if you actually look up these words in the *Oxford English Dictionary*, the supposedly upper-class ones sound very much cruder:

Sweet (Middle English). 1. That which is sweet to the taste; something having a sweet taste. b. A sweet food or drink.

Pudding (Middle English *poding* deriv. unkn.) I. 1. The stomach or one of the entrails of a pig, sheep or other animal, stuffed with minced meat, suet, seasoning, etc., boiled and kept till needed; a kind of sausage. II. 1. A preparation of food of a soft or moderately firm consistency, in which the ingredients, animal or vegetable, are either mingled in a farinaceous basis or are enclosed in a farinaceous crust. . . Preparations of batter, milk and eggs, rice, sago, suit-

64

ably seasoned and cooked by baking, are now also called puddings. . . .

But the classes at either end of the scale really don't give a damn. The noisiest soup-shlooper I ever heard at a dinner table in my life was the late Randolph Churchill. Once I spoke at the dinner of the Newport (Monmouthshire, i.e. practically in England) Literary Society. My overnight host, and a very kind one too, was the late Lord Raglan. Over breakfast, learning that I had worked for a short time in an advertising agency, he said 'Ah, I've always thought that must be very interestin'. I suppose it's really just a matter of thinking of a few *sloggans*?' Such was the conviction with which he pronounced this word that I half thought that was how you *should* say it.

It is true that you can still get books on etiquette which reflect a formality now gone for ever. In one by Lady Troubridge, revised as late as 1972, it says, of At Homes, 'it is unnecessary to write the name of the guest on the card, or to name the hour, as from 4 to 5.30 is recognised as the correct time during which to pay such visits,' and 'it is a good plan to inform the nearest cab rank that a dance is in progress, and thus save much telephoning'. On the one occasion where there still does have to be some formality and a correct order of doing things, a wedding, so many people want to do it right that there is still a steady sale for little books that tell them.

But really, if people aspire to anything in the way of a social manner, it is influenced as much by a kind of showbiz, mid-Atlantic easiness as by any attempt to be U; surely before the war it wasn't customary, as it now is, for hosts to kiss any opposite-sex dinner guests whom they know at all well when they arrive, and for everyone to call everyone 'darling'? Probably some kind of dividing line, still, occurs with the fork. The higher up you get (or the more American) the more you seem to be expected to eat everything with a fork. And of course many enigmas do remain. There are those, even now, who think it's somehow smarter to add the milk to the tea (I mean even when it's their own tea, so they can't be accused of not consulting someone's wishes as to how much milk); and for some reason it is perfectly OK to scatter pepper over your food but you mustn't scatter salt, you're supposed to make this dreary little heap at the side of the plate, where it all runs down into the gravy (sorry, *sauce*). Why? Pepper a scarce oriental spice so not to be wasted? Scattering salt an insult to the cook? (Pepper an individual choice)? Salt something ancient, Biblical, originally placed ritually on a plate? As for vinegar, it's never seen on U tables. 'Pass the condiments' will get mini-snob laugh; yet perfectly good word, from *condire*, to season—or *embalm*. Appropriate; maybe yesterday's U is today's non-U. Be blowed to that. Have vinegar with chips, scatter salt if you feel like it. Especially if you're a socialist peer.

Paul Jennings

RTHUR KOES[T...] Hungarian int[...] who has neve[...] been forgiven b[...] English intellec[...] (a) being cleve[...] they are, kr[...] about science a[...] literature and [...] ing personally experienced the h[...] totalitarian Continental gaols, cho[...] land as his home because, 't[...] Orwell, these crowds, "with their[...] mild faces, their bad teeth and [...] manners, this nation of flower-lov[...] stamp-collectors, pigeon-fanciers, [...] carpenters, coupon-snippers, darts[...] and crossword-puzzle fans lived [...] muddled ways, closer to the tex[...] invisible writing than any other[...]

Nowadays the teeth are better [...] and bingo-playing and telly-v[...] might be added to his list, and t[...] ners aren't quite so gentle in in[...] relations and on the roads (bad). [...] still a fair judgement. Belgians are[...] pigeon maniacs, but the long-[...] pigeon record is still held by the [...] Wellington. We have ¾ million [...] (which means about 22 million [...] quite a lot of them young men; [...] English have an infinite number [...] ways of keeping sane, i.e. knowi[...] to *do* in your spa[...]

Paul Jennings

HUNTIN, SHOOTIN AND FISHIN

CTUALLY, huntin, shootin and fishin have reached a kind of equilibrium in Englan now. Some say that Thomas Boothby of Leicester (1677–1752) hunted the first fox hounds in Englan. Typical, saying yer hunt a pack; jus somethin to fool the outsider who would naturally say yer hunt *with* the pack, it's the fox yer hunt. On the other han, yer don't hunt the Cottesmore or the Pytcheley or any of the posh hunts in The Shires, yer do hunt with them. Of course yer can hunt in Hunts or Hants or anywhere in Englan if yer've got the time and the money—there are over two hundred fox hunts, not to mention three stag hunts; but The Shires technically aren't just any old shires, they are Leicestershire, Northamptonshire and Rutlandshire. An of course the Belvoir, pronounced *Beaver*, counts as bein in The Shires although it's in Lincolnshire.

In the old days huntin was closer to war an danger an, well, what yer can only call masculinity, yer didn't have all these gels doin it (don't misunderstand me, they ride jus as well nowadays); an they hunted bigger prey, like wild boar an that.

Well, boars went out an foxes came in when huntin became the main occupation of the landed gentry (lot o land pinched from the monasteries after the Dissolution, o course, an monks didn't hunt, although o course they had fishponds, but that was only for anglin, presumably on Thursdays for the Friday fish—not proper, gentleman's fishin, no good startin that unless some uncle or perhaps even yer father taught yer in boyhood how to tie flies, cast, an all that, on long holidays by some distant, expensive river mos likely not in Englan at all, but Scotlan or Wales). The eighteenth and nineteenth, those were the golden centuries. Even now, every other old inn has a series o prints in the dinin room or on the stairs

showin comic mishaps, parson's hat an wig comin off, squire bein thrown into ditch on other side of fence.

Well, everyone said when the railways came it would be the end but not a bit of it, they made it easier for fellers to get out of town for weekend huntin, perhaps especially fellers wantin to climb socially a bit. The nineteenth- and early twentieth-century *Punch* is full of jokes on this theme, e.g. caption under drawin of a grouse moor:

> The Major: Cheery greeting that old boy gave you. Who is he?
> The Merchant: Oh, a great friend of mine. I shot him three times last year.

BLACK VELVET CAP.

Nowadays it's very different, the tide has receded, leavin the huntin, shootin and fishin set very much as it was before the railways came, let alone the motor car. On the whole they can get on with it just as they used to, except maybe when, in the case of huntin, packs of students sometimes come out with chemicals that destroy the scent, and of course every now and then there's an argument on the television between one of these students an a man in very good tweeds who says the fox enjoys it an anyway it steals chickens an if we didn't hunt it we'd have to shoot it an anyway farmers do shoot it an anyway why should you spoil other people's pleasure an anyway you look at huntin people an you'll find they understand, an are in communion with nature ·not like townees. But times changin. *The Gentleman's Diary* (Collins) used to be full of h., s. and f. dates, now it has blurb callin this 'delightfully useless information.' Met a huntin chap only the other day, he said 'all that "Plant a Tree in 73" stuff, dashed useful to the country as a whole; first generation to do this for ages, the Victorians didn't plant trees: but jolly good for huntin too, makin good coverts.'

Paul Jennings

It's nice to sit and think and fish,
And fish and sit and think,
And think and fish and sit and wish
That you could get a drink.

A KILL WITH THE DEVON AND SOMERSET STAGHOUNDS

71

ODDER GAMES

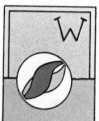

WHEN it comes to devising competitive ways of throwing, hitting, flipping through the air or pushing over various surfaces an infinite variety of globular or circular objects, you can't beat the English. Here is a tiny selection of the things they play when they're not playing football and cricket.

'What is dwile-flonking?' asked the magistrates of Bungay, Norfolk, not unexpectedly, when faced with a request for an extension of opening hours in the pursuance of this sport in a pub. After they have swallowed their beer the Waveney Valley and District Dwile Flonking Association have their tongues in their cheeks when they speak of ancient traditions, of manuscripts discovered that give the rules. The way they play it, a team of eight men stand in a circle, one of the opposing team stands in the middle with a bucket of ale, a flannel which he dips into it, and a pole called, believe it or not, a driveller, from the end of which he flicks the ale-sodden object, hoping to get three points if he hits one of the eight in the face, two if on the chest, one for below the belt. If he misses altogether *he* loses three points unless he can empty a chamber-pot full of beer. A simple and enjoyable pastime.

Many of the odder games are, in fact, refinements and formalizations (and highly skilled versions of) games played by children. Knur and Spel is a grown-up's version of the divinely simple boys' game known in midland streets as tip-cat, in Cumberland as piggy-stick. The boys have a six-inch stick pointed at both ends on the ground; they hit one end with a longer stick, so that it flies up into the air where, if they have a good eye, they hit it again. In Yorkshire and Lancashire the men have an iron spring-loaded contraption (the Spel) which throws a little porcelain ball (the Knur) up into the air, and they clout it with a long-handled mallet. The game is simply to see who can hit the farthest (two hundred yards is not uncommon). Each hit is called a rise, and a match usually consists of five, ten or fifteen rises.

The World Marbles Championship is played on a raised concrete ring outside a pub called The Greyhound at Tinsley Green, Sussex, apparently about fifty feet underneath airliners coming in to land at Gatwick. Each player has his own cherished tolley (often lovingly ground from an old lavatory pan) with which he tries to knock the forty-nine marbles off (he flicks it with his thumb and can impart a back spin so that his tolley stops dead after hitting the marble). This is the ver-

sion known as Ring Taw; there are others with names like Fortifications, Three Holes, Handers, and Arch Board or Bridge, which is a kind of Thumb Croquet.

Croquet itself is now very much an English-speaking game, although it has French ancestry. We have eighty registered clubs, with probably around two thousand members—apart from the unknown number who play on vicarage and other lawns. But it doesn't do to think of it as a vicarage-lawn game; what country do you suppose has more croquet players than England. France (French name, after all)? Italy? Some dreary old-civilization country? Not at all. Australia, that's what. After all, it's really a very bloody-minded game in which pleasure in your own skill takes second place to your ability to stop your opponent from doing anything at all. Basically, you have to get through six hoops and hit the winning peg. If you hit an opponent's ball (making roquet) you have the right to take croquet—put your ball next to his, move it to where he doesn't want it to be, and yours to where you do. If you're good enough you can make breaks as in billiards.

All the same, to most people who play croquet, quoits is probably something you play with rubber rings on A Deck during the cruise. Not so in the north east of England. Tees-side shipyard workers, miners, North Riding farmers, play it with iron rings weighing $5\frac{1}{4}$ lb. which are thrown eleven yards at a peg, the hob, set in a square yard of moist clay. You score a point with a ringer, but here again the skill lies in shots with names like pot, back pot, hill gater, Frenchman, in which the quoit lies in a position making it impossible for anyone else to get a ringer. An East Anglian version uses quoits of 8 or even 12 lb. and the distance is eighteen yards; tougher but not so precise as those Yorkshiremen, who can place the quoit almost as if they'd done it *in situ*.

You're not likely to find a miner playing Real (which means Royal) Tennis. There are only seventeen courts in England, and one of them, at Hampton Court, is the oldest place in the world where a ball game is still played. You would need more leisure than a miner has to have time just to learn the incredibly complicated rules (no wonder Lawn Tennis, which we invented, in 1874, supplanted it). You only serve from one end, and your serve has to bounce off the sloping roof of a kind of bicycle shed called the penthouse (with openings called galleries) into a prescribed area. Your opponent can set up a chase against you from his end (the hazard side) by getting into various galleries or rebounding near the back wall (behind which is another opening called the dedans, and he can get a point by hitting into

that, *and* you also have love-15 type scoring), then when he's serving to you it's up to you to set up a better chase against him, and . . . well, no wonder they play it at universities—proper, *old* universities like Oxford and Cambridge; it's like highly athletic chess.

Stoolball, played a great deal by ladies in Sussex, has the same rules as cricket, except that an over consists of eight balls, the wicket is a foot-square board on a stake, the bottom edge being 4 feet 8 inches above the ground, the bats are like bumper ping-pong ones, and the game is about four times as fast as cricket. In the one I saw, the Haywards Heath Bluebells beat the village of Barcombe; starting at seven they made 174 for 7 wickets declared, got their opponents out for 111, and after tea in the pavilion it was still light as their coach left.

Of course the English invented cricket at much the same time as they invented industry and the modern world; in fact cricket, for all its recurring drama, effort and tension, has long stretches of *nothing*, it is an artistic formal way of doing nothing for three whole days, and lots of our games are nothing if not leisurely. To play shove-ha'penny, all you have to do is sit in a pub and slide little discs into each of eight lateral divisions before your opponent does. It has ancestors in shove-groat and shove-penny, and shuffle-board. And God preserve us from its ever being called shove-half-p.

Not surprisingly, the indoor games, especially in pubs, are all pretty leisurely (though not skittles, which involves hurling a heavy wooden 'cheese' down a long alley). But they need skill You can see old boys in Sussex pubs swinging a ring suspended from the ceiling on to a hook in the wall, go after go, and miss it yourself all night. 6 million people play darts (more than any other sport); 25,000 of them actually buy *The Darts World* every month.

Let the great and ancient university of Cambridge have the last word. In 1955 their Tiddlywinks club was formed. In 1958 they played the Goons in Guildhall, London, and formed the World Tiddlywinks Congress, to which nobody came except other English people, although there are American teams now. The big disc, with which you flip the others (on a mat one yard by two, of a felt material) into a cup, is called the squidger, and if you get your wink over an opponent's, you have squopped it. The president at the time of writing is a mathematics graduate, called Alastair Duncan, who has had a letter from, among others, Moscow University, saying 'we are examining this game with interest'.

Paul Jennings

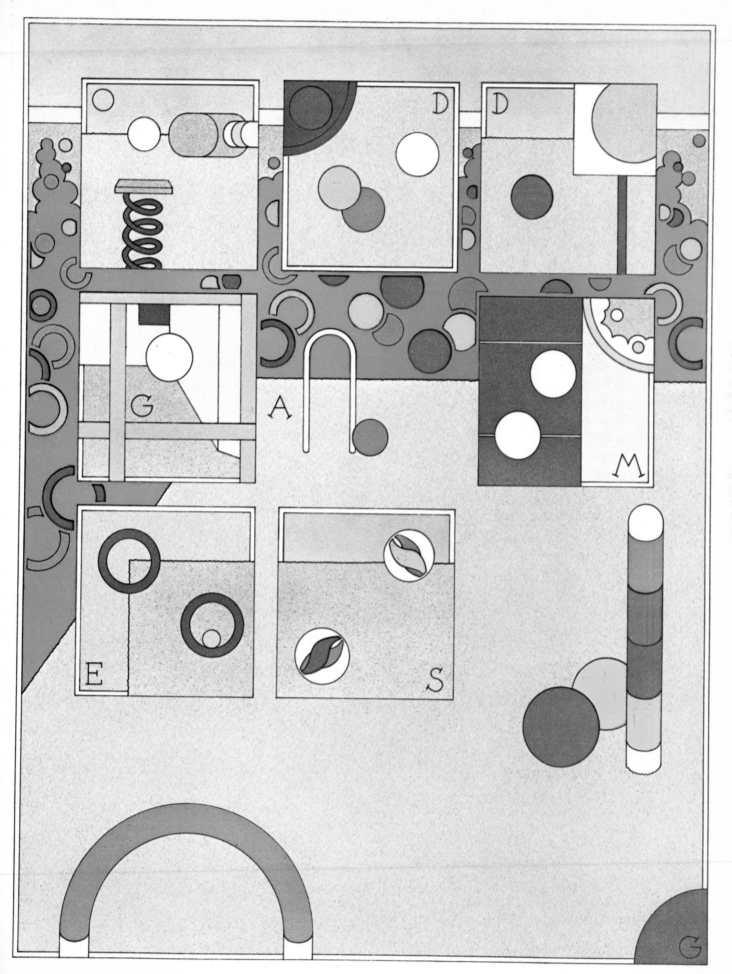

COME OUT TO PLAY

I IS only necessary to watch two schoolboys playing conkers—the careful aim, the cry of 'Strings!' when a mis-hit causes inter-twining or of 'Stamps!' when the weaker conker has broken and the broken pieces may be stamped on—to realize that children's games are very serious things.

As Stella Benson, who had been observing some child fellow-passengers on board ship, wrote in a marvellous *New Statesman* piece many years ago.

There is no such thing as youth, except in comparison with age. Children in the presence of children are not Little Things at all; they are more appallingly mature than we, the middle-aged, ever dare to be. Left to themselves, the children on board played deck games with an austerity seldom showed by their elders; they were pedantic abiders by the rules of the game . . . two sane and serious little boys, proceeding down the deck by means of a series of painful collisions, were heard by me to converse as follows: 'Hit you before you can say Jub. Jub-jub. I hit you first. No you didn't. Yes I did. No you didn't. Yes I did. No you didn't. Jub. Penny for a Jub. Dirty liar! Well then, that's seven-pence. Sevenpence halfpenny. Half-penny, hawpenny, huppeny. Yapenny, yawpenny, yuppenny. Hit you for a shilling. Can you talk like this: Smile Smit you for a smiling? (Appreciative laughter). Smilling. Smilling. Smelling. You're a smeller. Smeller yourself. Hit you for a smeller . . .'

Games cover the whole range of human behaviour, from appalling cruelty and ganging-up on some newcomer or natural outcast to prodigies of imagination. Indeed, any parent knows that expensive mechanical toys bought for Christmas or birthdays usually last about eight days. Quite often it turns out to be just *one* day. The thing that seems to give most pleasure is the big cardboard box that the groceries come in, which does duty as a house, a Dalek, a ship, a car . . . it doesn't matter, they make it up as they go along. Once, charmed by the sight of two small girls playing peaceably with their dolls which they had put in a hole in the ground with some sticks over the top, I asked them what the jug of water was for. 'They're in prison,' they said, 'we're giving them horrible drinks.'

But basically of course games are devoted to the serious business of amusement, of enjoying life, a duty which is laid on us all and progressively forgotten as we get older. (Any fool can be serious. As

Chesterton remarked, 'it is easy to be heavy, hard to be light. Satan fell by the force of gravity.')

Like everything else nowadays, games have been the subject of some pretty serious research. Obviously the basic ones are as old, or perhaps one should say as young, as mankind itself. It is well known that there were Greek and Roman versions of Blind Man's Buff and Tag (or Tig, or Catch, or whatever its regional name is). Equally obviously there is a Janus quality, looking both backwards and forwards to events or people that have stuck in the national consciousness. A lady in Ipswich wrote to the local paper wondering if anyone remembered a sequence-game she had played as a child with the words

Queen Queen Caroline
Dip your hands in turpentine
Turpentine will make them shine
Queen Queen Caroline

She was deluged with scholarly replies about that sad wife of George IV, shut out from his coronation, and her cortège passing through East Anglia. There are those (*Chambers' Encyclopaedia*, to be exact) who say 'Here We Go Gathering Nuts in May' is a survival of primitive marriage by capture.

Maybe, maybe. And maybe in centuries when ours is a dim past instead of the dim present it is now, there will be new rhymes:

I had a little sterling
And nothing would it buy
Not a silver dollar
And gold was much too high
The King of Zurich's baillie
Came to visit me
All for the sake
Of my sterling currency

Or perhaps De Gaulle's rebuff of Heath's original assault on the Common Market will be skipped or danced to:

Edward went to market
Knocked upon the door
Charlie took his basket
And knocked him on the floor

'The old seasonal games have almost vanished,' said the WI village scrapbook of Willoughby, Lincolnshire. 'The primary schoolchildren had never seen the old wooden tops, nor knew how they were whipped. Those who hoarded marbles did not know how to play with them. Inquiries about iron hoops brought *one*, blacksmith-made, out of its hiding place . . . some sort of hopscotch survived . . . all skipping games were rare. . . .'

Yet Pembury, near Tunbridge Wells, near London, had a plentiful stock of skipping and ball-catching rhymes

Plainsy to America, plainsy to Japan
Plainsy to Old England and plainsy back to land

Plainsy hullabaloo, plainsy hullabaloo
Plainsy plainsy plainsy plainsy hulla-baloo.

Donald Duck
Washing up
Broke a saucer
And a cup

It is true you never see boys whipping tops. But then you never see children playing the game known as Fivestones in the midlands, Jacks or Jack-stars in the south. All the same, H. P. Gibson & Son of London sell millions of them. Only the metal stars, now, they say. The ceramic cubes with which one went through the ritual (throw one, scoop up four, catch the one on the back of the hand, then throw two, etc.) aren't made any more. Nor can you get the beautiful striated glass alley tors (they came from Bohemia) which lorded it over plain marbles; it all comes from the Far East now.

Games, like laughter, have a beautiful madness and irrationality, somehow combined with deep, deep reality, that escapes all scientific classification (stuffed though modern psychology is with 'Theories of Games'). You can see on the face of a child deep in a game the kind of total absorption observable in the figure of Pythagoras, *Thinking*, carved on a portal at Chartres. Absorption in the real has come full circle. (Though all know it as children, few know it as adult geniuses). It would be tempting to speculate that, though children the world over play games, it is the English who, sensing the Death of God, once did unconsciously try to preserve religion in their untranslatable phrase *playing the game*. But that would be Games Theory too.

Games are a persistent, unkillable, junior partner of mythology. But they go on as they always have done. The mysteries of the world are approached with the same healthy mixture of the ordinary and the miraculous ('If you see a dandelion you will want to pee,' they think in Hampshire. 'If you see an ambulance, hold your collar until you see a four-footed animal,' they say in Lincolnshire). No wonder the standard work, *Children's Games in Street and Playground* by Peter and Iona Opie has an index of twenty-six pages, starting with *A pennorth of chips* and *Acker, backer, soda cracker* and proceeding by way of *Ally Ally Onker, Bad Eggs, British and Reds, Bumeroo, Cabbage Tit, Dreaded Lurgi (The), Grandmother's Footsteps, Hur-ly Burly, Thump on the Back, Jacob Where Are You?, Jimmy Knacker, Le-Oh Queen-ie-Ball, Rum-stick-abum, Spitfires and Gliders, Squeak Whistle Holly, To Beccles to Beccles, Tracking Twenty, Buzz Off* and I know not what else, to *Zig Zag Zooliger.*

Paul Jennings

THE LYKE WAKE WALK

TO QUALIFY for the Lyke Wake Club you have to walk straight across the North Yorkshire moors in twenty-four hours, from their western edge at Osmotherley to Ravenscar by the sea, halfway between Whitby and Scarborough. You have to keep to the summits, which means that in these tough forty miles you will have climbed five thousand feet.

It has been done in the time by a clergyman on his eighty-first birthday, by a boy of 7½, by a man in a dinner jacket and top hat carrying a briefcase, by a party of Durham policewomen and by three artificial inseminators from the Cattle Breeding Station at York.

On the other hand another man who tried it couldn't get out of his bath without assistance, and was off work for seven weeks. One glance at the map will show you it's not as easy as all that (unless your name is Arthur Puckrin; he did once across in 6½ hours, twice in 16 hours 17 minutes, and *three* times—that's 120 miles—in 32 hours 15 minutes. Beginning to slow down, you see.)

Anybody doing this incredible thing is alone for hours at a stretch with space, air, wind, heather, and lost-sounding birds, like a soul in transit. And that's one very good reason why the walk is named after the famous Cleveland 'Lyke Wake Dirge', with its haunting refrain 'An' Christ tak up thy saul'. The dirge was sung while the corpse (lyke) lay in the house, while a candle remained lit and the fleet or flet (the embers) burned. The physical details of the grim moorland scenery are used to express the hazards of the Judgement:

This yah neet, this yah neet,
　Ivvery neet an' all,
Fire an' fleet an' cannle leet,
　An' Christ tak up thy saul.

When thoo frae hence away art passed
　Ivvery neet an' all
Ti Whinny Moor thoo coms at last
　An' Christ tak up thy saul.

If ivver thoo gav owther hosen or shoon
　Ivvery neet an' all
Clap thee doon, an' put 'em on,
　An Christ tak up thy saul.

But if hosen an' shoon thoo nivver gav
　　　　　　　　　　　　nean
　Ivvery neet an' all
T'whinnies'll prick thee sair ti t' beean,
　An' Christ tak up thy saul.

Frae Whinny Moor, when too art passed
　Ivvery neet an' all,

Ti t'Brig o' Dreead thoo cums at last
　An Christ tak up thy saul.

If ivver thoo gave o' thy siller an' gowd,
　Ivvery neet an' all,
On t'Brig o' Dreead tho'll find footho'd,
　An' Christ tak up thy saul.

But if siller an gowd thoo niver gav neean,
　Ivvery neet an' all,
Thoo'll doon, doon tummle towards Hell
　　　　　　　　　　　　Fleeames,
　An' Christ tak up thy saul.

Frae t'Brig o'Dreead when too art passed
　Ivvery neet an' all,
Ti t'fleeames o' Hell tho'll cum at last,
　An Christ tak up thy saul.

If ivver thoo gave owther bite or sup,
　Ivvery neet an' all,
T'fleeames'll nivver catch thee up,
　An' Christ take up thy saul.

But if bite or sup thoo nivver gav neean,
　Ivvery neet an' all,
T'fleeames'll bon thee sair ti t'beean,
　An Christ take up thy saul.

The Lyke Wake Club was formed in 1955 by Bill Cowley, a Yorkshire farmer who issued a challenge to anyone to do the walk in twenty-four hours. The group that accepted actually did it in thirteen hours, and the club was formed there and then, with Mr Cowley as its Chief Dirger. Over the years they have built up a fine lugubrious tradition for their annual dinners (better known, naturally, as Wakes), with officials such as the Melancholy Mace Bearer, the Horrible Horn-blower, the Cheerless Chaplain and the Sorrowful Shroud Supplier. The menu is likely to contain items like Broiled Cock Howe Cockerels on the Bone, Cringle Moor Crisps, Grilled Howe Sausages, Sil Howe Salad, Blue Men i' t'Moss, Simon Howe Surprise and Bloody Beck Disaster. Women members, who wear a black scarf with the club badge of a silver candle and two tumuli on a black coffin, form the Circle of Witches, and 'their duty,' says Mr Cowley, 'is to cast suitable spells and ward off the machinations of Hobs, Boggets, Gabriel Ratchets and the like.'

To become a Master (or Mistress) of Misery (black neck-bands) you must do three crossings, one of which must be in the opposite direction, and attend two Wakes. To become a Doctor of Dolefulness (purple bands) you must do four, one of them alone and one of them between 1 December and 28 February (when you really *might* die if you didn't know what you were at) and present a thesis.

Not surprisingly, these are very happy and convivial gatherings. It probably does seem funny *after* you've done it.

Paul Jennings

THE COUNTY SHOW

O H, PAPA, *see what a lot of people are queueing at the entrance to the County Show. Let us hurry, for I fear that we shall not be able to get in.*

Have no fear, my child. Although it is true that the attendance of 2,563,000 at fifty county and national agricultural shows in 1972 was the best for six years, an advance of 200,000 on the figures for 1970, this was only a partial regaining of lost ground.

Is it possible that even larger crowds once attended the County Show than the animated throng which now presses about us?

Indeed, yes. The animation which you observe derives partly from the strong urban admixture among the visitors: many of them driving from the town in their cars, have no personal interest in agriculture as such, and you will see that they give no more than a cursory glance at such exhibits as the miniature tractor imported, I understand, from Rumania, and sold at a price only made possible by heavy subsidies on the part of the Rumanian government, or at demonstrations of new electrical aids to pig husbandry. For them it is a holiday, all the more so for giving them a whiff of country atmosphere.

Is it for such visitors that such extra attractions as the hot-air balloon ascent are arranged? I must own that it is the principal attraction for me!

I trust you will not be disappointed, my child. The intrepid aeronauts will not be able to fill that great globe of orange nylon with air heated by the propane burner (in essence nothing more than a huge blow-torch) if the wind rises any higher than at present, as I fear it may.

But, whatever the elements, we shall surely at any rate be able to see the tent-pegging contest between two teams of the Royal Military Police, the one on horseback and the other on motor-cycles?

Yes, nothing but a truly torrential downpour would prevent that, and you would not be disappointed, as you were of another aerial spectacle last year, when the Red Devils, the famous display team of the Parachute Regiment, were prevented from performing by the inclement weather.

Pray, Papa, were not county shows of the past comparatively dull affairs before such thrilling entertainments were provided?

You must not commit the common error of supposing that country folk and farmers are dull people who only foregather for serious purposes, my child. From times immemorial their meetings have been marked by a merry conviviality. There would have been, perhaps, such contests as the tug-of-war, or climbing the greasy pole, and long before the air was filled with music from loudspeakers attached to poles there would have been local bands in attendance. In short, the show would have been less formal and commercial than it is today. Yet one thing has remained constant. Can you guess what it is?

I think perhaps it was the judging of the livestock.

Yes, you are quite right. You will remember from your history lessons that English farming was revolutionized during the eighteenth century by such figures as Jethro Tull, inventor of drilling and horse-hoeing (making land more productive), 'Turnip Townshend' and Coke of Norfolk who were pioneers in the various crop variation and rotation that led to a great flexibility in English farming after centuries of unchanged and rather wasteful methods. These, together with livestock pioneers like Robert Bakewell, made farmers aware of a need for *efficiency*. And the competitive show-exhibition is a powerful means of giving them standards

of efficiency at which to aim. The first Smithfield Show was in 1799, and you will find that some of the county agricultural associations, which organize these shows, go back to those times. Indeed the Royal Lancashire was founded even earlier, in 1767, and the Bath and West in 1777. The Newark and Nottinghamshire dates from 1799, like the Smithfield, and very many of them go back to the early nineteenth century, such as the Suffolk (1831) or the Leicestershire (1834).

Wherever I look I see technical devices and literature which I am too young to understand. Yet surely even the skilled farmer of today would be hard put to it to absorb everything in one short visit?

It is in the recognition of this very fact that the Royal Agricultural Society maintain a *permanent* exhibition at their National Centre, near Kenilworth, where inquirers may at any time study such things as farm electrics, dairying, specialized herds, pigs, and the like, as well as visiting *the* Show, the Royal, in July.

Is the promotion of these shows the only function of the agricultural societies, Papa?

By no means. The stated aims of all of them contain such phrases as 'the improvement of agriculture, horticulture, forestry and allied pursuits, and the development of husbandry', and nowadays a third or so of their membership may not be actual farmers but those con-

cerned with the ever-developing range of farm machinery, or with soil and plant science. They arrange lectures and demonstrations. They hold 'farm competitions' in which visiting judges assess farms and the skill with which they are managed. But it is probably true that the county show is still the crown of their year. It is certainly the time at which the general public are most aware of them. And you are quite right to suggest that the judging of livestock is the real focus of interest. Indeed it attracted the attention, although perhaps not in a strictly scientific agricultural sense, of a poet called Stevie Smith (who in spite of the name was a woman). She wrote a celebrated poem called 'The Best Beast of the Fat Stock Show at Earls Court'.

Can you recite it, Papa?

Alas, I can remember only the last verse:

I touched his hide
I touched the root of his horns
The breath of the Beast
Came in low moans.

We will look up the rest of it when we get home. It is in the *Guinness Book of Poetry* 4, I am almost sure. Meanwhile, before the Royal Mounted Police begin, I believe we shall be just in time to see the end of the sheep-dog trials.

Oh yes, Papa, it must be over there, where all the people are lining the rails. Yes, oh, see, what a clever dog! He has got all the sheep into that little triangle of hurdles.

All except one. See how he lies flat on the earth, and how his master communicates with him merely by a low whistle. What long hours of training that must take.

Ah, see, the silly fool sheep has run away, all his work will be ruined. If I were the dog I should give the sheep a sharp bite.

That is not the way to speak even of sheep. Now you will see how they get that one sheep back without losing the others.

It is quite Biblical is it not, Papa?

I doubt if the words which the farmer is now saying under his breath are Biblical. But come, I am sure you will also be interested in the demonstrations of country crafts near the largest marquee. Some, such as cooperage and the making of wooden wheels, though fascinating to watch, are now only of antiquarian interest. Others, such as thatching, are assured of a future as long as people desire to live in our beautiful thatched cottages, their roofs carefully trimmed and layered in eastern England, more moulded to the houses in the west. And there are still many village blacksmiths who—but what is it, why are you pulling my sleeve?

Dad, Dad, can we go on the dodgems? Can we see the balloon? Can we go on the swings? Can we have some sweets? Can we . . .

Paul Jennings

79

THE SPORTING WEEKEND

FUNNY thing really: the Greek for leisure is *schole*, from which the word scholar. Slaves got on with drawing water, hewing wood, the world's work, gentlemen studied and thought. That's what leisure meant; spare time for the mind.

Not in England though. Thought is too much like work. It was in England that leisure first came to mean, above all else, sport. We were the first nation where great industrialized masses were shut away from the air all week, in mines, in the first factories and mills. And we were the first to dream so deeply of the weekend as the time for bursting out, into the open air, for communal-competitive games, on the green grass.

As well as Manchester cloth, Birmingham brass, railway engines, we exported our weekend sports to the world. It may have outstripped us, our games at home may have been commercialized and pressurized, spectators may outnumber players, sport for millions may have become something between police serials on television. But there are still enormous numbers for whom the weekend means do-it-yourself sport.

And you've only got to look at the name of the game to see an ancient, ancestral English rightness, something from deep in the racial subconscious where words are

formed. The Latins may have Real Madrid and Benfica and Pele; but the word *futbol* cannot, in the nature of things, mean to them what 'soccer' means to us.

Just hear the word. Does it not sound like a game? Jack and Dick are soccer players. Quick, Jack, crack a corker goalie-shocker! The cocky, stocky, padded-stocking soccer players hack and kick and head like mad. Stop him, Dick. Take a crack, tackle quick, quick flick-pass to back, or take a corner, quirky luck! Plucky, lucky, stocky soccer players.

At the weekend Dennis and Glenys play tennis. Tennis teas nice and nifty. Neatly the net is tensioned, torsioned, what fun is in Janice in tennis togs, Tinling-inspired with frillpants and furbelows! Smashlob crosscourt, cucumber sandwich, tennis in Sanderstead, Surbiton, singled and angled to baseline. Or two serious singlesmen sweating and smashing in shorts.

Wimbledon-Hambledon axis of summer (Hambledon birthplace of cricket) from tennis to cricket, breaking for tea. O jiminy cricket! He snick it. He knock it! He block it, he pick it, he smack it, he crack it, he whack it. He *snick* it, a wicket! Wicket-gate, church gate, lych gate and riches of summer, the elms and the dreams, with leg bye bye-bye snoozem and lose 'em in deckchairs. Bat on ball bowlable, white on the green the summery scene for musing and dozing, sixty for six O cricket he snick it, he's OWZAT he snick it, awake at the wicket, he's OUT.

But rugger is rugged and dogged, for sloggers and sluggers in winter, dug in the heavydown, heavedown heel, haul ho ho scramble and scrimmage. Thews and thighs and banded jerseys, fair and foul, barrelchest bullyboys, bawling a bathsong, where will the grog be, where will the Jag be, hair of the dog be for hairy rugby wallahs and fellers? Nothing is stronger or bigger than rugger.

Paul Jennings

SOMETHING ABOUT A DAME

I T PROBABLY wasn't until the Second World War that we realized there was anything extraordinary about pantomimes at all. It was after the war that a revue contained the famous sketch in which an English dowager explains the intricacies of it all to an incredulous GI. ('No kidding? The guy is a Dame, and the dame is a guy?') Even now, they're the most taken-for-granted, enduring part of the British theatre. There are hundreds of thousands of people for whom the pantomine was the first experience of live theatre; for lots of them, now taking *their* children to this stubbornly surviving, incredibly trad hotch-potch (heartily despised by Shaw and other intellectuals) it is the only theatrical experience of their lives. The pantomime opening on Boxing Day and finishing some time around the appearance of the first almond blossom, is to some performers what the month of August is to seaside landladies—the busiest and best-rewarded time of the year.

The secret is that there's no intellectual rot about a pantomime. It is pure theatre, full of pure and simple emotions ranging from terror (which can be quite real to a five-year-old when the Demon King or the Giant appears), delicious laughter (when the Broker's Men get busy with the wallpaper or the custard pies), pathos (when Buttons realizes that Cinderella is not for him) to the deep, lovers-reunited, all-come-right-at-last, everybody-smiling sequined finale.

Heaven knows it has an intellectual enough history. Pantomime means, literally, 'imitating everything', and there were famous ancient Roman chaps who did just that (and the tradition of silent mime has come right down to Charlie Chaplin and now, Marcel Marceau). Then it came to mean a kind of mythological ballet. It was introduced to England in the eighteenth century mixed up with the Harlequinade, developed into an after-piece and light relief put on *with* serious plays, weakening their impact and, in many theatres, ousting them as they developed into an elaborate extravaganza full of transformation scenes, water scenes, all the tricks of the trade. The rhyming-couplet, trad fairy story pantomime that we know today took its final form (or so it appears at the moment) in Victorian times. There's not much left of the Harlequinade now, but there are plenty of mysterious traditions if you know where to look for them. For instance, the tradition that the evil characters—Demon King, King Rat, and the rest—come in on the actors' left, and the Good Fairies and angels or whatever come in on the right, goes back to the medieval mystery plays.

Of course, it's also an infinitely flexible form, perfectly capable of absorbing pop stars, variety artists or mere television personalities, not to mention jugglers, acrobats or dancing fountains. It is also deliciously corny. A line I cherish is one that I heard the Prince, in a hunting scene in *Cinderella* at Brighton, utter to a kow-towing innkeeper in a green baize apron. 'Tell me, good innkeeper,' she said, slapping her shapely thigh, 'have you a room where we may change our wearing apparel?'

In this same pantomime the immortal Jimmy Wheeler, as Baron Hardup, came

upon his daughters, the Ugly Sisters, making up a huge parcel. It was a seventy-five-piece tea set with which they hoped to influence the Prince. 'Yer not goin' to send that through the post, are yer?' he enquired. 'Yer know what they do with it. First of all, they STAMP on it, like this' (Furious thump on parcel, sound of breakage.) 'Then they THROW IT ON THE FLOOR, then they JUMP on it, like this . . .' It was five minutes of pure destructive joy.

Pantomime is also supremely flexible in the way it can be put on by anybody, from the slickest professional company of nationally-known stars to the scout group, the bank, the school and (perhaps most frequently of all) the village.

At one end of the scale, all the subtlest trick photography, illusion and 'graphics' that television can command were used in the TV presentation, by The Goodies, of what must surely have been the most surrealist *Mother Goose* ever, involving among other things, a *Jeu sans frontières* in which anybody falling into a pool of piranha fish came out as a skeleton, a giant, owner of the golden-egg layers, who was not a giant at all but the rather small Alfie Bass with a megaphone, and geese that could dive bomb with their golden eggs.

At the other end there is the village pantomime in which only the bare outline of the plot would be intelligible to the stranger, all the jokes in the script being about local personalities. In the Memorial Hall at Wonersh, near Guildford, they've been doing a pantomime since 1959. It's always a sellout, for ten days, and 75% of the profits go to the Hall fund. One family has five members in it. Script and music are by an accountant, Peter Osborne (his parents live there but he works in London and comes down every year for it). A stranger would doubtless recognise the outline of the *Dick Whittington* story although the laughter when Dick stammers 'but, but, but . . .' and is met with the reply 'no buts here except at the off-licence' would mystify him unless he knew that the local off-licence is kept by Mrs Eileen Butt.

Fred Rome, a famous pantomime script writer in his day, had the knack of really awful pantomime jokes. From *Babes in the Wood*:

BARON: You watered the celery with red ink and hoped it would come up rhubarb.
DAME: Don't be so *red-ink-ulas*.

From *Dick Whittington*:
FITZWARREN: Well, 'ere I am on 'ighgate 'ill. Whenever I come to 'ighgate 'ill I get well. I love to be in the country and sniff the ozone from the radish trees.

From *Aladdin*:
ALADDIN: I'm so hungry I could eat anything.
TWANKEY: Well, why not *bolt* the door?

Incidentally, Twankey comes from *twan-kai* a kind of green tea; more tradition.

Perhaps the core of the pantomime's appeal is its unique audience participation. 'Oh yes I will!' says the Demon King. 'OH NO YOU WON'T!' squeal a thousand delighted childish voices. 'There isn't a gorilla, children, is there?' 'YES!' 'There isn't.' 'YES THERE IS!' 'Where is it then?' 'BEHIND YOU!' No wonder they are so ready to sing the song louder than the rivals on the other side of the audience. No wonder the parents smile. Nothing has changed.

Paul Jennings

COVENT GARDEN OPERA HOUSE
General Manager . . . C. A. BARRAND
"ENGLAND'S ORIGINAL HOME OF PANTOMIME" . . . G. C. REYNOLDS Secretary

On Monday, December 26th, 1938, at 2.0 p.m.
AND EVERY EVENING AT 7.30
FRANCIS LAIDLER'S MAGNIFICENT PANTOMIME
"RED RIDING HOOD"

A NEW SUPER PRODUCTION
A CARNIVAL OF FUN
PANTOMIME AT ITS VERY BEST

MATINEES at 2
DAILY during the first 4 weeks and afterwards every WEDNESDAY, THURSDAY and SATURDAY

ON, ON, ON WITH THE DANCE

THE RIGID Victorian etiquette of English dancing started to disappear about 1910 when first the exotic Argentine tango arrived in London via Paris and then ragtime music from America developed the two-step into a wild one-step. A little later, during the First World War, foxtrot music was heard in this country for the first time and the great change was about to begin.

When professional teachers were at last drawn to this free and unfettered style of dancing, it was suddenly realized that when people from different parts of the country met on social occasions their steps were so different it was almost impossible for them to enjoy dancing together!

The largest and most influential professional organization in those days was the Imperial Society of Teachers of Dancing which was mainly concerned with ballet and other forms of dancing, but in 1924 they invited some of the leading London ballroom dancers to form a ballroom branch of the society. Technical committees were formed and the stage was set for the English to lead the world in ballroom dancing, a lead which they have now maintained for fifty years.

The first countries to come under the spell of what was fast becoming known as the English Style of dancing were Denmark and Germany and shortly afterwards, South Africa and Australia. Understandably the last to succumb were the Latin countries and America, whence so much of the music and some of the dances originated. In fact for many years the very affluent dance professionals in the United States were very anti-English-Style and it was not until the early sixties when the Imperial Society sponsored a number of lecture-examination tours to the States that an 'English style' branch of the society was permitted to operate. Now English Style takes its place alongside American Social Dancing and the World Professional Championships were staged at the Madison Square Gardens in New York in 1973.

Ballroom dancing today consists of two completely different styles. The Standard or 'Modern' dances are the waltz, foxtrot, tango, quickstep, and, for international events, the Viennese waltz. The Latin dances which developed more slowly and certainly with more national and international controversy are the rumba, samba, cha cha cha, paso doble and the jive.

It was as early as the thirties that English dancers heard about the rumba and other Latin dances but they were completely apathetic. The teachers argued about the steps, the rhythm and the exotic hip movement but little progress was made. The coming of Jitterbug warned us that the Americans had rhythmic ideas far beyond our comprehension and when, during the last war, the top American

bands came to this country, one felt the wind of change! About this time, a well-known English teacher was asked to judge a waltz competition at an American servicemen's club in London. The standard was appalling but afterwards when the band played a swing number the Americans crowded the floor with their English partners and danced with a rhythmic feeling and musical interpretation never seen in this country before. The story goes that the teacher suggested he should judge a swing competition and eventually kept them all dancing for nearly half an hour while he was trying to learn the steps!

The Cubans or Americans with their inherent sense of rhythm have produced many wonderful rhythms and dances and it is strange but true that the sober Anglo-Saxons are able to develop these exotic and passionate dances and do them so well that the originators now travel thousands of miles to come to England to see and to learn how to perform their own dances!

The Official Board of Ballroom Dancing in this country, which sets the tempo of the dances, makes rules to govern competitions and tests and the system of judging them, is flattered to find that practically every national and indeed international body in the world has adopted these rules.

The first Palais de Danse was opened in England in 1919 at Hammersmith. It was

'palais' idea really caught on when Mecca Dancing opened a chain of similar halls throughout the country. Thus the scene was set for over twenty years. Boy met girl at the palais. The middle-aged and even the elderly made their weekly visit to enjoy social dancing or to practise the steps they had learned at the local dance school, and everything was very respectable. But in the early sixties the twist, the

the scene of the Tory congress). For a week or ten days competitions in Modern and the Latin dances are held every night. culminating in the prestigious British Professional Championships on the final night. Nearly 50 percent of the entries are from overseas.

Last year the winners received twenty-five pounds for each dance they won! These are people who are paid very large fees to demonstrate and teach in Japan, Australia, South Africa and at least two dozen other countries. They could earn far more from one demonstration than they do in a week at Blackpool but the title is one of the most coveted in the world and to win it pays very good dividends. Not all championship organizers are quite so parsimonious. Mecca Dancing give a thousand-pound first prize in each section of their United Kingdom championships and also contribute between two and three thousand pounds for the winning couples to compete in the World Championships when they are held in faraway countries such as Japan, Australia and the USA.

Once beginners pass their Bronze Test they are hooked! They study for the Silver, Gold and Gold Bar or Star and some struggle on to their Supreme Award. At least 65 percent of the people who take these tests are women. In some areas the percentage is higher. The really keen dancers find a partner and join the competition scene and years later may be seen on the 'Come Dancing' television show. The majority just continue to attend 'practice classes' and feel happier and a little superior when they join their friends at the annual masonic, rotary or sports club dance. Now that the palais shows signs of discarding or at least minimizing the influence of pop they will be seen once or twice a week at the local palais enjoying one of the most pleasurable social recreations available.

Meanwhile, hundreds of thousands of middle-aged (and above) dancers who have been completely unaffected by the pop scene will be attending dances run by their 'Old Time Dance Club' now rather misnamed as the dances they enjoy most are the 'Modern Sequence Dances'.

These dances, usually set to sixteen bars of music, include all the most glamorous figures which a professional would take months to perfect. But the stoic English 'Old Timers' have no qualms at all. They dance the X Line, the Eros Line, the Rudolph Fallaway, the Stutter, the Woodpecker Taps and the Kangaroo Hops with complete confidence and nonchalance. And who but an Englishman could do that!

an instant success and attracted many keen dancers who had previously danced at the smart London hotels. An American innovation the 'pen', provided the lonely or partnerless patron with a professional partner for sixpence a dance and quite a number of famous professionals started their dancing life in the Hammersmith pen. It was not until the thirties that the

music of the Beatles and disco dancing completely changed the scene.

The palais is a truly English institution. Only Australia has been able to copy 'life at the palais' with any success.

The one institution that no country in the world has been able to copy is the Blackpool Festival, held in May every year at the huge Winter Gardens (often

And who but an Englishman would go on a dancing cruise holiday to Gibraltar— or even to Japan, just to dance—and to compete against the same couples who are his rivals at Birmingham and Battersea every other weekend!

Alex Moore

85

POP

OR TEN years, since the Beatles emerged from their cavernous existence in Liverpool, British groups have been significant, trendsetting, influential makers of popular music.

When Rolls Royce tumbled, sleek businessmen were still jiving to Led Zeppelin in Tokyo hot spots. When strikes paralysed our industry and exports, German and Swiss financiers were still booking tickets for the latest super group from England. And if ever world war looms again, the young soldiers of opposing nations may well peer nervously over the earthworks and call in conciliatory fashion: 'You like the Rolling Stones? Ceasefire!'

As a trained observer in these matters, even I have been surprised to find that in America, Australia, Japan and Borneo, there are natives collecting British rock albums where once they bartered for beads, trinkets and cooking pots. In savage, downtown New York for example, Led Zeppelin, most formidable of 'heavy' bands, first played there in 1969 to a screaming army of fans who knew as much about the lyrics of the songs, and the development of thematic statements, as any of their most ardent hometown admirers.

On the Trans-Siberian Express, David Bowie is still mentioned with awe after he entertained the peasants en route for Vladivostock during his 1973 world tour.

Some English bands have worked so often along the flightpath between Los Angeles and New York that they are firmly believed to be American, until they order tea, sausage and mash, with chips in brown gravy at the Holiday Inn. Some Americans claim they recognize British musicians by their neglected teeth.

Says Ron Mael, US songwriter now resident in London: 'The secret of English bands' success is rotten teeth. Everybody thinks it's their boots, or some mystical heritage. But it's definitely not the boots. If you ever have a better dental service then the English balance of payments will be in a lot worse shape.'

There is a mixture of skilled engineering and gentlemanly amateurism at work. For the spirit that moves our music makers is the same that fired the brains and brawn of yeomen like George Stephenson, or even Isambard Kingdom Brunel (albeit an adopted foreigner). They pluck from the air a dazzling concept, and lo—we have the Clifton Suspension Bridge, or Emerson, Lake & Palmer's light show.

They took the rough-shod concepts of R & B and transfused with them a variety of local influences. From rural Andover came the Troggs, who were so green when they came into pop that their amiable leader Reg Presley claims not only did they have straw in their ears, but 'lettuces, cabbages and carrots'. And yet they launched a farmyard rhythm so violent and sensuous on their hit 'Wild Thing' that Jimi Hendrix, noted for his own brand of wildness, was moved to perform a cover version.

Stackridge, decidedly rustic gents from Somerset, with names like Mutter Slater and Billy Bent, perform a brand of music which is influenced by Delius, and has been hailed as 'pastoral rock'. One of their finest arrangements is a piece called 'God Speed The Plough' which would have been warmly welcomed by Will Cobbett as light entertainment during one of his interminable rides.

From the north of England too, bands have developed. Lindisfarne in Newcastle took the country by storm with their earthy Geordie poetry, and rhetoric frequently directed with great bitterness towards the moguls of rock, or further afield, the property speculators and town planners who run amuck in their cities. Their music, while appealing to the hardcore rock audience, is deeply infiltrated with the folk dances and jigs of their native heath.

In the smoky midlands, the lads of the industrial townscapes have donned their boots and scuffled out of the grinding inevitability of life in a factory, and soared to the heights in working-class bands; Mott the Hoople, Slade, Led Zeppelin, Traffic, Black Sabbath, the Moody Blues, the Move and Roy Wood's Wizzard.

And in London, great magnet for all the nation's aspiring talent, and the south in general, there have emerged gifted, trained and well-heeled rock musicians, whose smooth techniques and sophisticated artistry have enriched our lives. Keyboard players like Keith Emerson, Rick Wakeman, Jon Lord and Dave Greenslade, have inspired eulogies in the serious press and performed with the finest orchestras and choirs in specially composed symphonies and concertos. Indeed the London Symphony Orchestra was so impressed with the piano playing of Rick Wakeman, who normally plays Moog synthesizer, Mellotron or Hammond organ with Yes, that they invited him to play a Mozart piano concerto at the Royal Festival Hall.

A far cry from the clanging dustbin lids of Stackridge, or the wheezy harmonica solos of Lindisfarne, but just as typically English are the Kinks, who started out life as an R & B band and became instead a vehicle for the poignant, bitter-sweet songs of Ray Davies, the petulant, but sensitive lead singer. They grind into performances with all the vibrancy of a threshing machine on the verge of a seizure. But they can inspire love and affection, particularly in America, where on a 1972 tour, audiences called out 'God Save the Kinks'.

The gentlemen of Yes retire to their hotel rooms after a concert to practise, write more music and consume health food. Not so The Who, a group internationally famous for their wild abandon, on stage and off. Not for them the Swedish style orgy, or the liberated love feast. However they indulge in an English, eighteenth-century sort of fun, with ribaldry, pranks and endless japes.

Ian Anderson of Jethro Tull can convert audiences all over the world, by a mixture of wit, stage craft and musicianship. Dressed usually in a cod-piece and tattered dressing gown, prancing about with a flute at his lips, he is a markedly intelligent and sensitive musician.

While a rock'n'roll band might appear to the casual, disinterested observer as a disorganized bunch of incompetents, Genesis are the antithesis of this concept. Four of them are ex-public-school boys, while the fifth, their drummer, Phil Collins, is an East Ender. Here the two class structures meet with mutual benefit.

Their songs, expanded into long arrangements, give scope for exceptional use of dynamics, light and shade, key and time changes, and a wide range of instruments, powder flashes, and finally the wires and harness which whisk Peter Gabriel, their shy, stuttering but courageous leader into the roof at the climax of their show. Genesis have created a supramusical entertainment without parallel in theatre or rock music.

Emerson, Lake & Palmer too have incorporated spectacular devices to enhance their show in a tasteful and exciting manner. A stunning beast, half tank, half animal called 'Tarkus' has long been a part of their act, glowing in baleful red light, and emitting puffs of smoke from its gun barrel.

David Bowie became the first rock and roll singer to dare appear as nature certainly did not intend, wearing a flowing lady's dress. 'It's not a woman's dress, it's a man's dress,' he averred later.

The dress soon gave way to a wide range of ambivalent, revealing attire, until Bowie seemed not of the human race, but a beautiful creature from another galaxy. Even his backing group were titled The Spiders from Mars and, out on the streets, fans were painting their faces with streaks of lightning, in an expression of solidarity. The 'British Way' succeeds where perhaps other 'Ways' fail, in NOT having a 'Way'. All ways are possible and accepted in moderation.

Chris Welch

MAKE MINE A PUB

THE SECRET of the English pub, ignored at their peril by the designers of new pubs with 'theme' bars (cotton, millers with sacks of grain, Spain, cars, Famous Beauties, fishing, I've seen them all, or a lot of them anyway), and concealed lighting, and black leather, and whatever the latest interior-decoration gimmick might be, is *subdivision*. Just as the English landscape itself is a miracle of getting more into one little valley—a village, a lake, a park, woods, bit of heathland, cul-de-sac of magic cottages leading to a bridgeless stream, fields, secret inns, church, maybe *three* churches, shop with bearded chap making marvellous tweed, farms, sawmill, blacksmith, small electronics factory—than is possible by strictly physical measurements—so is the English pub, all under one roof (or collection of roofs added higgledy-piggledy over the centuries), a miracle of subdivision.

It's easy enough to shove a purely sociological label on to this—a big bleak plastic-tile-floored public bar for the proles with their great pints slopping over on to the counter, the saloon bar for the chaps in check tweed jackets and their experienced-looking women (or young men in sharp purple suits with their dollies), the lounge for married couples on a slow-drinking, ruminative night out, etc., etc. And there are people who will tell you about Victorian-style pubs (still found in great numbers in any city), and the reason for the rows of little opaque glass panels, set on vertical pivots, which can be swung so that they blot out the view, across the barman's working area, from the posh bars to the prole ones. These panels, they say, date from the days when the indentures of apprentices forbade them to drink. They would be in the public bar, the master would be in the saloon bar, each would know the other was there, so they would turn the little panels round so that neither could see the other.

This may or may not be true, but it misses the point, which is that in an English pub you can be with a group of your cronies, whether this group be large or small, in a uniquely-shaped comfortable part of a house. Not a hotel; a house. And since England is a northern European country, a *warm* house, just like your own, preferably with an open, visible fire.

Recently we've found out about the 'Continong', pavement cafés, all that stuff. The English pub has always had a garden at the back (the best ones anyway) where you could have a drink with the

kids on a Sunday morning; but now this side of it has been developed, and the more advanced ones have these round white tables outside, with striped umbrellas.

And very nice too—especially if there is lapping water, whether of river or canal, in sight. We might as well take advantage of the sun when it does appear. All the same, the basic English pub is one where although they do consent to shove a couple of benches outside in the brief capricious summer, life is fundamentally geared to the heart-warming, social draught imbibed on a winter, autumn, or cold spring night, in a bar which may be labelled the Public, the Private, the Saloon, the Lounge, the Smoking room (although I have yet to see a non-smoking room), the Bar Parlour, the Ladies (!) or most deliciously apt of all, the Snug. Not to mention the part where you come to buy the stuff to take home, called either with a kind of legalistic dreariness the off-licence or, more humanly, The Jug and Bottle.

And God bless us, what centuries of tradition, of heraldic splendour, of mad English quirkiness, are evoked by the names of our pubs! Never mind The Red Lion, The White Hart, The Trip to Jerusalem (in Nottingham, a memory of the Crusades), The Britannia, The King's Head. Think of that pub in Chatham called The Ordinary Fellow; it was so named after King George V had remarked to the Archbishop of Canterbury, during his Silver Jubilee, 'I like to think of myself as just an ordinary sort of fellow'.

Lots of people will tell you that The Cat and the Fiddle (the one at Leek, Staffs. is claimed to be the highest one in England) is a corruption of *Catherina Fidelis*, a pious medieval reference to St Catherine. Others tell you that it refers to one Caton, a staunch Protestant in Queen Mary's reign, who earned the nickname '*Caton fidele*'— a likely story, about as likely as that The Goat and Compasses is a corruption of God Encompasseth Thee. There are far more extraordinary transmutations.

The Lyre and Swan (the badge of the Society of Musicians) became The Goose and Gridiron. A pub in Sheffield called

The Iron Devil (appropriate, one would have thought, in view of the local industries) was originally The Hirondelle (the swallow, device of the Arundel family). One G. J. Monson-Fitzjohn, in *Quaint Signs of Old Inns* tells of an inn sign The Andrew Mac, showing a kilted Highlander, being cleaned to reveal underneath the title The Andromache.

You can eat in pubs too. The seventeenth-century traveller Fynes Moryson wrote:

The world affords not such Inns as England hath, either for good and cheap entertainment after the Guest's own pleasure, or for humble attendance on passengers, yes in very poore villages, where if Curculio of Plautus should see the thatched houses, he would fall into a fainting of his spirits, but if he should smell the variety of meates, his starveling look would be much cheared.

There was always a better time, and some of today's keg beer helped on its way to your glass by gas cylinders instead of the landlord pulling the handle which pumps it from barrels knowledgeably tapped and stored is a long way from (to quote Ivor Brown) our ancestors' 'leather bottle. Their bombards, gaspins, black jacks and piggins sound like a powerful company'. All the same, either for a convivial round, or a quiet pint with a nice cheap plate of Shepherd's Pie or a quick salad, in a cosy, shut-in little space, it's the pub.

Paul Jennings

O, I DO LIKE

THE quintessential English seaside town has a promenade with railings that feel knobbly where the umpteenth coat of green paint has covered the rust, a quiet terminus station with a lot of wood, glass and greenish light, places for clock golf, putting greens, streets with graceful cast-iron pillars supporting a kind of veranda over the pavement, shops with many frivolous goods on stands and in cases outside, hanging in doorways—beach balls, rather tasteless sweets made to look like pebbles, many hats and other objects made of straw; climbing back streets with little houses having cards saying 'Vacancies' in narrow stone bay windows, an intricate-legged pier with brown water slopping up and down barnacled struts, many precise flower beds on little greens, a posh end with blue-and-white hotels containing turkey carpet and brass stair rails and many cream doors, a vulgar end terminating in a harbour, fish parlours and pubs that seem to open at

11 a.m., steps to a cliff top path, a solemn hydraulic cliff railway, an Edwardian Catholic church called Star of the Sea hidden in a side street, a bandstand, chalked blackboards announcing boat trips, a back-town area of hollow oily garages, bus stations, a grammar school and Victoria Park with boating lake, many deck-chairs of green canvas occupied by people with open-necked shirts and mild tans, donkey-rides on the beach, and sand-sculpture competitions organized by national newspapers. And a little grass aerodrome from which you can take a ten-minute flight. And open-topped buses. And shops full of rock. And ice-cream parlours with green wicker chairs. And a pier show, and a summer repertory company. And, many, many children in sandals and Aertex shirts . . .

The Pavilion Rockeries by Night, Bournemouth

And it doesn't exist any more.

Of course, you may find many, or even all of these ingredients in plenty of seaside towns; but, like all works of art, the perfect English seaside town was not really recognized as such until after it had passed its peak of social usefulness and function. The whole point of it was its

wedding-cake impermanence, with all that wood in the architecture, a suggestion that even the hotels were glorified beach huts, that nobody lived here during the winter.

First there was the fashionable Regency sea-bathing, Brighton developing from Brighthelmstone, and the marvellously stagey, correctly impermanent-looking Pavilion (still so, after all these years). Pavilion, paladin, promenade, parokeet, these are summer seaside words, as Edith Sitwell realized so brilliantly:

Beside the sea, metallic bright
And sequined with the noisy light,
Duennas slowly promenade
Each like a patch of sudden shade;

While colours like a parokeet
Shrill loudly to the chattering heat,
And gowns as white as innocence
With sudden sweetness take the sense

Those crested paladins the waves
Are sighing to their tawny slaves
The sands . . .

"SORRY, MISTER!"

There followed the railway age, bringing the sea, for the first time, within the reach of the majority of people who, although they had for centuries known themselves to be a maritime race, had spent all their lives in dreamy inland shires, or even more, in grimy industrial cities. From these cities and from London the clanking commercial steam network, now wearing a face of pleasure, for the first time offered *everyone* the privilege of mobility which, in all previous ages, had been the privilege of the aristocrat with horses (after all, the aristocracy often got its very name from the horse; the *equitatus* of Ancient Rome, the *Ritter* or Rider of Germany, the *Chevalier*, the *Cavalier*, the *Caballero*).

Those many-liveried trains, those locomotives with copper bands round their funnels, brought the crowds to places where the line must stop; on an embankmented station where they stepped out into salt winds and the wild cries of gulls, or into a sober terminus at the back of what was already a town, where once there had been just a few fishermen.

They came perhaps for Bed and Breakfast—English phrase, incorporating our informally ceremonious, unhurried, day-starting meal, with full time to relish it for once, on holiday; not perfunctory bread and coffee, but porridge, eggs with bacon or boiled or scrambled, toast, marmalade, and of course tea. In whatever once-only-visited house, enough for a memory lasting for ever of high flubby beds in rooms with dark wardrobes, marble-topped wash-stands with matching jug, ewer and soap dish, against a light blue or white wall-

paper patterned with small flowers, later pasted over the bulging wooden strip covering the wiring for the new electric light; of anfractuous stairs, of gulls heard on waking, the early morning search for a newspaper on the Promenade, magically empty as yet, by a sea glittering with promise, or Wagnerian-wild . . .

Or they came to Rooms, this family at this table, that family at that, with their own sauce bottles. Sandy wet bathing costumes on window-sills. One of the Rooms containing a piano, folding card-tables (only later, a radiogram) fan in the grate, sets of Dickens; curtains blown gently through open summer windows, causing a shimmering of the subaqueous Sunday light.

But it was not a place where they thought of living permanently. Drawn by the restless sea, infinite, yet with its unarguable, final straight-line horizon, somehow saying to them 'there's nothing after this, this is the end', they evolved a style of life for a week, or a fortnight (or a day; ah, the handbills in midland stations; 'Rhyl Excursion, 7/6'; '8 hours in Blackpool, 8/6!') which celebrated impermanence. When the leaves fell they would all have turned back from this brief exposure, thrilling and disturbing, to the infinite sea, back to the cosy inland business of working, living, procreating.

No doubt there was something deep and ancestral about it too, the call of the sea-womb from which we all emerged. 'Agassiz, Simroth, Moseley and other authorities', says an encyclopaedia, 'incline to the idea that the littoral was the original home of life, and it is almost irresistible to consider it the testing bed from which life is passed to higher forms in the sea, the air, or on land. Sir John Murray has especially emphasised the importance of the "mud-line" at an average depth of 100 fathoms, where minute inorganic and organic particles come to rest and form the great feeding grounds of the ocean. . . .'

So your true seaside had, as well as the sandy shore for bathing, the bit with rocks, the lines of the strata obstinately at awkward angles to the direction of the incoming waves; with soft, trailing, green sea-moss, countless little pools, tiny claws scuttling, making a small, sandy commotion in clear

water; with huge heavily-waving knee-deep seaweed-forests, or bladder-wrack dried in the sun, popping under youthful plimsolls. You took bits of it home, it told you how the weather was going to change, although only after it *had* changed anyway.

Such was the place for the magic day, week, fortnight. Once in a year, remembered, looked forward to, but not part of everyday life. Small wonder that its visible forms were all of defiant, feather-

weight, summertime frivolity.

> And see the children sport upon the
> shore,
> And hear the mighty waters rolling
> evermore.

There could be no such thing as a seaside cathedral.

But almost before we realized that this delicate, airy, lacy, sandblown form, the English seaside town, had been thrown up, a shape in the spray for a fraction of a second, two things happened.

First, municipalization. Suburbs crept over sea-heath skylines; trolley buses came, and grammar schools, and shopless avenues of bungalows for retired people; and civic centres, and winter tea-time music, and ice shows; and even factories. The holiday is the great modern secular escape from *ennui*, the only vision of something Other, but now many holiday places became suitable subjects for the immortal couplet of Osbert Lancaster

> Heard on this coast, the music of the
> spheres
> Would sound like something from *The
> Gondoliers*

Second, the motor car. Not only can people buzz down to the seaside whenever they like, the fact that many of them have wider horizons, often in the Mediterranean, gives to our own seaside towns a faint cul-de-sac air; nowhere to park either. The true, far-off, faery quality had something to do with arriving, just for this special occasion, if not by train, at least

in a charabanc, or a 1930s car, breasting the last hill, suddenly seeing this flat green field with white flecks, stretching to a windblown nowhere. Chesterton tells somewhere of a child seeing the sea for the first time and being asked for his reactions. After a long pause, during which the asker remembered all the images and adjectives which have occurred to poets, from Homer's 'wine-dark' to Keats ('perilous seas, in faery lands forlorn') and beyond, the child says 'it's like a cauliflower.' The green stalk of the curving breaker as it rears up, the flower of froth at the top; a brand-new fresh-minted metaphor.

Now it is the mid-seventies, smelling of petrol, the pier-show sketches are full of references to television stars, there are holiday camps where drying wet clothes is no problem because there's no need to *get* them wet. All the same, here and there, at eleven, or seven in the morning, by the cockle stall, on the beach, in the deck chair, hearing the shingle late at night, for children, for the first visitor, here it is. The English seaside.

Paul Jennings

SINGING IS SO GOOD A THING

THE white and gold tiers of the Teatro Regio, the magnificent opera house at Parma, Italy, had been freshly painted for the celebrations in honour of Verdi, born 150 years previously in the nearby village of Buseto. His passionate and tender *Requiem* was drawing to a close before a packed audience. The performance was also being relayed to an overflow audience in a nearby church. There is a marvellous peace at the end of this work. After the thrilling terror of the great fanfares representing the Last Trump, the huge double-fugue chorus glorifying God in the *Sanctus*, the eloquent solos pleading for forgiveness and mercy, comes the last quiet, heartfelt page. The soprano soloist, as if praying by herself, breathes *libera eas, Domine, de morte aeterna*—'deliver them, O Lord, from eternal death'—while the chorus murmur behind her.

The music died away into a throbbing stillness. There was a tranced moment, and then a pandemonium of cheering broke out. The audience flung down hundreds of red carnations plucked from the gala decorations. At last the conductor, Carlo Maria Giulini, stilled the fantastic ovation by raising his baton for an encore. An encore, in the Verdi *Requiem!* Unthinkable in London's Festival Hall, but this was Italy. The chorus sang the great triumphant *Sanctus* again.

But what was a British chorus doing, taking Verdi to Italy—surely the supreme musical version of coals to Newcastle? After all, Parma audiences are known and discussed with bated breath wherever singers gather. They are no respecters of persons; if they don't like a performance they make it perfectly clear.

They went because they were invited. And they were invited because the traditional, and still growing, love of choral singing has produced several choirs with an international reputation. And there is certainly no lack of foreign invitations. Since 1958 the famous Huddersfield Choral Society, a pioneer of these excursions, has been to Vienna, Brussels, Berlin, Munich, Oporto and Boston (Mass.). The Royal Choral Society has been to New York, the Bach Choir to Milan. The New Philharmonia has an annual date with the Spanish National Orchestra in Madrid. 'The best choir in Europe,' said the newspaper ABC, 'they performed a thousand feats of true virtuosity.' Each time they go the Spanish government cheerfully pays for charter aircraft and several days' hotel accommodation for two hundred people.

This is simply because air transport has now made the logistics, if not the expense, of moving two hundred people to a distant city much more simple than it was when Huddersfield made their first trip abroad, by train and boat from Harwich to Amsterdam in 1928. But the reputation has been there for generations. Foreign trips, for those lucky enough to live in the musical north of England, or in London, which has at last caught up, are the icing on the cake, the top of the pyramid.

The body of the pyramid consists of some eighty thousand choral singers who come together to make music in societies all over Britain, from Yeovil's, with seventy-six members, to Lerwick's (in the Shetlands) with forty-seven. Some 622 of these are affiliated to a central body, the National Federation of Music Societies.

Few things are as life-enhancing as singing. Often, after a hard day's work, the prospect of sitting on hard chairs in a bleak rehearsal room and working with intense concentration, mental and physical effort combined, for two or three hours, does not seem an inviting one. But any choralist will tell you that although you might go in feeling tired and dispirited, perhaps even with a headache, you come out feeling entirely rejuvenated, with a kind of resonant feeling in your head and chest. You can't move for three hours on the highest peaks ever reached by the human mind, in stupendous works like Bach's *Passions* or *Mass in B Minor*, or the *Messiah*, or Beethoven's breath-taking *Missa Solemnis*, (only in our day beginning to reveal itself as the Everest of music), without a sense of exhilaration, of the mind being stretched.

But there's more to it than that. There's a harmony *beyond* the heard harmony of music, a mysterious intimation that this is how human life is meant to be lived. Each person finds himself the more he finds the community of the chorus. All these diverse people from so many walks of life assemble —and when the conductor's hand is raised, what a miracle it is, that mere physical human breath should be turned into this spiritual communion!

No wonder the old pictures of heaven always showed the angels as singing or playing instruments! Music, that's the divine art, as Schubert observed. You don't see the angels hacking away at carving, or painting pictures or writing poetry. They make music.

Playing instruments is for professionals. But anyone with a reasonable voice can join the elect in a choir, very often for a joint performance where artistically he is on equal terms with the professionals of the orchestra (and where else would an amateur, tormented by the sight of piano scores that he will never be able to play, totally ignorant even of what fingers you

use on the flute or the violin, get to be on the same platform with Klemperer, Giulini, Davis?).

Each voice or instrument makes its statement, but instead of following each other in time, as statements do in a mere conversation (I say something, you reply, I reply . . .) they are *simultaneous*. So in one sense we are already liberated from time.

Yet there is no shouting down. Even while making our statements we are *listening* to the curves of other voices' lines, we damp down when they have an important entry. We are intensely aware of each other as a body. It is pure democracy. If only we could get a bit more of it into our social and political life!

Three-quarters of a century before the Huddersfield Choral Society was founded in 1836, John Wesley wrote of the town 'a wilder people I never saw in England.' Such was the unpromising background against which it began as a self-bettering, do-it-yourself enterprise by local working people, run by a committee under a foreman. Each member was allowed 'three gills of ale, and bread and cheese &c.' (more than any singer gets today). There were only sixteen of them, and they met once a month to practise each Friday on or before full moon, so that members could see their way home along the unlit roads!

Today there are 240 members (of all classes!), five concerts a year, recordings, foreign tours and a world-wide reputation. Members pay an annual subscription of a pound, although for such special enterprises as their trip to Boston each member paid sixty pounds. But with typical Yorkshire practicality a savings club was opened two years before they went, so that the most impecunious young soprano could manage it.

It is wrong to think of Huddersfield (or any other chorus today) sticking to *Messiah* or *Elijah*. They recently did *Alexander Nevsky*, a cantata of the music for the film of that name composed by Prokofiev in 1938; and that modern classic, Walton's *Belshazzar's Feast*, was written for Leeds.

Even the visual picture that many people have is out of date—the women all in long white dresses, or in some cases white for sopranos, black for contraltos. The ladies of the Royal Choral Society now wear a rather chic blue gown, and Huddersfield has gone even gayer; after all where should they know about textile design if not there? So Mrs Waring, who lectured in this subject at the local technical college, created for the ladies a pink dress, and very striking it looks (although local wits cannot now resist the temptation to speak of the Huddersfield *Coral* Society!).

Yesterday Yorkshire, today Yorkshire and the rest of Britain. Consider, for instance, what goes on just in London. There's the oldest of them all, the Royal Choral Society, with three hundred members. The Alexandra Choir (170) was another major body taking its name from a building, in this case the Alexandra Palace, opened two years later in 1873. There are the other choirs associated with big professional orchestras besides the New Philharmonia; the London Philharmonic Choir—the vital, predominantly young London Symphony Chorus.

Also in London is the BBC Choral Society, with 180 singers. It was founded in 1928, and one of its aims has always been to use the BBC's independence from at least some of the concert-promoter's financial worries to perform interesting but not always box-office works. Recently they've acquired a new young director, John Poole, and they attract a fair number of students and young voices. They have tackled such works as the *Transfiguration* of Messiaen, whom many think the greatest living French composer, or the *St Luke Passion* by Penderecki of Poland.

There is absolutely no reason why civil servants from the black-coat-and-pinstripe world of the Treasury shouldn't make music, but it struck *Punch* as a bit of a joke. 'It is rumoured that they are trying to perfect the Sterling Aria', quipped the magazine. In fact the Treasury singers share with the Board of Trade Choir the distinction of having sung in perhaps the most historic and beautiful hall in Britain—Westminster Hall. And they were in the same group of buildings as a very grand musical organization indeed, with a history of over two centuries. The Noblemen and Gentlemen's Catch Club was founded in 1761 and is still going strong. It has three dinners; with singing afterwards, each year—and where but in the House of Lords.

There are a vast number of occupation-based choirs. St Thomas' Hospital Music Society, for instance, has 140 members. The Barclay's Bank Musical Society gives two concerts a year to audiences of a thousand at the Queen Elizabeth Hall. There's the London Transport Choral Society, the Stock Exchange Male Voice Choir, the Bank of England Male Voice Choir. There's even a choir of twenty-five blind people, the Pro Canto Singers. There's the London Choral Society, the South-west London Choral Society, the London Orpheus Choir, the City of London Choir. There's the London University Choir, there are choral societies at Imperial College and even the London School of Economics.

Wherever life takes people in these islands they will never be too far away to join some group in which they can re-discover every week the truth so succinctly expressed by William Byrd in the sixteenth century about singing:

'First, it is a knowledge easily taught, and quickly learned where there is a good Master, and an apt Scoller.

2. The exercise of singing is delightful to Nature and doth good to preserve the health of Man.

3. It doth strengthen all the parts of the breast, and doth open the pipes.

4. It is a singular good remedie for a stutting and stammering in the speech.

5. It is the best meanes to procure a perfect pronunciation and to make a good Orator.

6. It is the onely way to know where Nature hath bestowed the benefit of a good voyce: which guift is so rare, as there is not one among a thousand, that hath it: and in many, that excellent guift is lost, because they want Art to expresse Nature.

7. There is not any Musicke of Instruments whatsoever, comparable to that which is made of the voyce of Men, where the voyces are good, well sorted and ordered.

8. The better the voyce is, the meeter it is to honour and serve God therewith: and the voyce of man is chiefly to be imployed to that ende.

Since singing is so good a thing
I wish all men would learn to sing.'

Paul Jennings

THE CASUAL LOOK

Inspire, O Muse sartorial, this song
About our fear of wearing something
    wrong;
Show doubters, in this free-and-easy day
When informality is here to stay,
The splendid oxymoron of our dress,
A formal informality, no less!
But, ere descanting on what wear doth
    please
The Briton dressing for his hours of ease
Show how mistaken was the oft-held view,
When Rt. Hon. Bevan, in a suit of blue
Waited upon his Queen, that something
    died
And England started on her downward
    slide.
That Minister of Health, who felt the urge
To help democracy by wearing serge
And hoped to see a wild idea take root—
The abolition of the morning suit—
Must surely marvel, from th'Elysian
    shade,
To see more men that ever thus arrayed;
At every wedding with pretence to taste
In morning suit behold the bridegroom
    graced,
On each long hair-do, an absurd top hat
(What would Aneurin Bevan make of
    that?)
One English firm will never make a loss,
Those well-known hirers-out, the Brothers
    Moss.
The Briton knows that all about him lies
A world where bridegrooms seem to wear
    black ties
(He sees their wedding photos; horrid
    sight!
Can all their weddings be performed at
    night?)
But here, no matter what the world may
    think
A *red* tail coat is known as hunting *pink*.
Note how the Briton (who *invented*
    sport)
Gave each game clothing of a
    special sort;
Not uniforms, but with
    more subtle air,

Mere adaptations of his common wear.
Thus, he plays cricket on the village green
Beneath tall elms, a timeless summer
    scene
Where squire (stockbroker) and rude
    peasant (clerk)
Ply subtle skills from 2 p.m. till dark
All dressed in garb unknown across the
    Channel—
White shirts, white *boots*, and trousers of
    white flannel;
Elegant game, in which the last disgrace is
Trousers not white (or even worse, with
    braces)!
Consider bowls, where over greens are
    rolled
Expensive spheres, by persons growing old,
    More cunning with each year;
        observe the Skip
            In flannels
                never baggy on
                his hip
            And crested blazer,
                which could well
                be worn
(And is) in pubs on
    any Sabbath morn.
(The ladies' dresses—

always cut like *that*—
    Are crowned, too, by a
        kind of trilby hat.)
    Though 'anyone for tennis?' is a
        phrase
Now used to cover all those pre-war plays
Where maids were comic on the telephone
And men's dress clothes weren't Moss
    Bros, but their own
There still survives about our leisure wear
Some trace residual of the open air;
    Thus 'hacking jackets', double vent
        at back,
        Are worn by thousands who
            will never hack
                (They often go with
                    'cavalry twill',
                        of course,
        On legs unused to any
            kind of horse.)
At soccer, see what hats and scarves are
    worn
Striped for the team to which support is
    sworn
(More ways than one!), and hear the lusty
    cheers
From men who haven't kicked a ball for
    years.

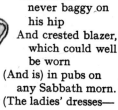

Now, no longer on an isle marooned
See Britain to a sterner world attuned
Where sport, a function of the sovereign
    State
Has better things to do than re-create.
In many forecasts for the human race
Leisure assumes an ever higher place
And think-tank men, in tones of gloom
    and woe
Tell us a thing we all knew years ago—
That now we have these shorter working
    hours
To reap their benefit's beyond our powers

If, with spare time our fathers never knew
We only say 'I can't think what to *do*!'
Here's the revenge of our technology;
Leisure itself become an industry,
An academic subject, with degrees,
For those who teach us to enjoy our ease.
Now leisure almost has to be defined
As needing clothing specially designed;
Thus, ski-ing now can simply not be done
(Although invented by Sir Arnold Lunn
In days when no one seemed to feel the
    need
For anything but good old British tweed)
By anyone unable to be dressed
In ski-pants, boots, windcheater, and the
    rest.

Rock-climbing now is
    never done by halves;
        They roll down special
        socks that show their
        calves;
    And people now who
        mess about in boats
Tend towards brilliant
    nylon orange coats.
In this new world
    mere pleasure in the
        game
        Makes modern
            players hang their
            heads in shame;
        In sport, like
            economics, not
            to win

Is now the only unforgiven sin.
Once we were football kings. Now
    (dismal scene!)
We are not in the World Cup last sixteen
(Though *this* decline, alas, was not because
We played all gaily and defied such laws.)
Is all then lost? Shall England toe the line
And hard-edged zones of 'work' and
    'sport' define.
And seek, like others in the EEC
In both a cold, supreme efficiency?
Ah! We came first (though now we're
    running late)
To look on leisure as a sportive state
And show in dress the scope of our intent.
The bowler hat proclaims the city gent
Who all weekend about the country roams
Wearing a back-and-front, like Sherlock
    Holmes,
A hat designed for stalking Scottish deer,
Though Haywards be the only Heath
    he's near.

This is the land, of field and tree and
    hedge,
Where life and sport own no dividing
    edge,
Where men, not following fanatic creeds,
For one thing do care still—their
    well-cut tweeds
And come what
    may, though
    Heaven itself
    be shook,
Still try to keep
    that English
    Casual Look.
Paul Jennings

5 THE POET Auden, in a
memorable phrase, de-
scribed us as having
'trousered Africa'—per-
haps not strictly true
when you see the colour-
ful garments worn by
African statesmen at
diplomatic parties, or
indeed in Africa, or London for that
matter. All the same, the sad uniformity
of post-Victorian male clothing did move
the sculptor Eric Gill to complain bitterly
of such sculptor's chores as carving boot-
laces and buttons on municipal statues. It
is only recently people have noticed that
in the army, in the town hall, and the
river, even in the streets, considerable
numbers of us have been devoting a great
deal of time and attention to Dressing Up.

THE HAXEY HOOD GAME

PEOPLE tend to forget about Lincolnshire, even though it's the second largest county in England. Huge empty fens, every other place-name ending in -by; Wragby, Saltfleetby, Sloothby, Willoughby, Dalderby, Thimbleby, Grimsby, Bealsby, Candlesby, Gunby, Somersby (where Tennyson was born, who knew all about long cold seas breaking on pale sands).

Haxey, in the Isle of Axholme (one of many British 'Isles' which are not really islands, merely areas circumscribed by rivers or dykes—the Isle of Ely is the best-known of them) is the place where they hunt for the Haxey Hood, in a mysterious kind of controlled riot of which the origins are as misty as the fading afternoon of every 6 January (Twelfth Night) when they play it.

Within a dozen miles or so of Haxey are not only Owmby, Kexby, Saxby and Snitterby but also such looming-out-of-the-mist names as Knaith, Wroot, Thorpe-in-the-Fallows and, perhaps most sonorous of all, East Lound.

Big-boned, no-nonsense men from places like that come every 6 January to Haxey; the Lord of the Hood (at the moment Mr Stan Board, who works in the council offices at Doncaster) and the Chief Boggan in hunting pink, with fantastically decorated tall hats, and the Fool, in motley with a painted face, and eleven other Boggans, in red shirts.

Top hats (however gaudily decorated) and mud, dressing up and scrimmaging, formality and vagueness—the bringing together of such opposites seems particularly appropriate in Lincolnshire (incidentally the very name from which

Lincoln comes—*Lindum Colonia*—is a reminder that here a Roman colony did indeed bring that classical southern order, a framework imposed on the chaotic wild north; the two sides of our character).

Elsewhere in this book you can see plenty of Old Customs, many of them involving the peasants dressed as gentry. Top hats very often figure. In the curious ancient Mumming Play in which there is a tremendous fight between St George and the Turkish Knight, the slain warrior is brought to life by a comic Doctor who is rarely complete without a top hat. What is special about the Haxey Hood (except that of course all such customs are special) is this combination of the dressing up with something really quite wild physically. Nobody wears a top hat, for instance, in the Shrove Tuesday football played through streets of boarded-up shop windows at Ashbourne, Derbyshire, and

several other places. They just get on with it.

But here, in Haxey, are these Boggans in their red shirts, with their Chief in his tall hat, all ready for a very rough game indeed.

Nobody is quite sure what the word 'Boggan' comes from, unless it's the mud they churn up in the pursuit of the Hood, which is a leather-covered cylindrical object about eighteen inches long. The whole thing is said to date from an episode in the late thirteenth century, when one Lady de Mowbray was out riding and her black silk hood blew off. Thirteen peasants chased it, and the hefty serf who won the free-for-all was too shy to give it to her, so a more enterprising companion (now the Fool) seized it and made the presentation. They all got half an acre of land, and devised the game of the Hood from the incident.

The thing starts with traditional songs ('The Farmer's Boy', 'Canons', 'John Barleycorn') and a pub-to-pub procession. Then the Fool (for the last five years a farmer called Peter Bee) makes a lasses-and-lads type of welcome speech. Then the Lord leads everyone to the fields—the supposed site of the original thirteen half acres; and there's a kind of preliminary when for half an hour or so dummy 'hoods', rolls of sacking, are thrown up for anyone to capture; later the Lord retrieves these for small sums of money.

The real business begins almost as dusk has really set in. The Lord throws up the leather-covered 'Sway Hood', which is instantly the centre of a heaving, shouting scrum of anything up to two hundred men. It really *does* sway—over fields and gardens, up and down the street, wherever its impetus takes it. In its time the Sway has dented cars, knocked bits off the church wall, and more than bent Mrs Perkins' pear tree. In fact for some time before Haxey Hood day they go round singing their songs in The King's Head and The Duke William and collecting as a cover against any possible damage.

Sometimes it lasts for hours. There are two opposing sides, of indeterminate size; and the goal is, literally, the pub, where the reward is free beer.

Otherwise there don't seem to be any rules. Here are locals, here are some lads from Leeds University who, like many others, dive into the thick of it and then come out for a rest, or to repair minor wounds. 'Man down!' comes a cry, and the mêlée parts for a moment for a man with a broken leg to be carried out. You'd think there'd be a string of ambulances waiting—but no, they have to phone for one. Phones, ambulances—they didn't have things like that when this game started. But there *is* a rule, after all. 'You've come on wrong day,' growls an old man called Walter (this is one of those occasions when you never hear a surname), who was himself a Boggan for forty years. 'It weren't a proper Sway at all. I saw 'em *throwin'* it.'

You're not supposed to do that. It's not rugby; people can play rugby anywhere. But there's only one place in the world where they play the Haxey Hood game.
Paul Jennings

BACUP AND OTHER DANCERS

NE of London's surprises. Millions know nothing about the National Folk Festival; but on a wintry Saturday afternoon, in the empty impersonal museum-frowning streets behind the Albert Hall, thousands who do know are pouring out of their parked coaches. Chattering lines of schoolchildren flowing up wide Victorian steps (they will do mass dancing in the arena during the interval: ponytails bobbing, much scrambling for Cokes, solemn eyes over straws); life swirling among cold monuments. Many adults too. Evening performance also sold out. You never read about it. It just happens, and they know.

In corridors and scruffy old changing-rooms with one old chair and broken shelves, riot of sound and colours, national costumes. Yugoslav practises haunting pastoral flute. Belgian team who wave and twirl huge flags in formation. Four darkly elegant high-cheekboned Scots who lay down bright swords with proud precision, dance neatly over them in black pumps, kilts. Brawny delicacy, graceful virility.

And, of course, Morris dancers everywhere. A pretty familiar sight these days, in all sorts of places—some natural and obvious, others not. Outside a village pub, performance advertised by a few modest do-it-yourself posters; chaps, some bearded, some clerkly, not at all peasant-looking, more like bank clerks (maybe some *are* bank clerks, why in hell not?), dancing to rhythm which may seem tame after disco but which few untrained disco types could sustain for ten minutes, let alone hour-long display, perhaps followed by two more at two more pubs. On the other hand, surprise, surprise, they have been seen enlivening a dreary concrete piazza of an undistinguished new office block hard by St Paul's, one summer evening. Surprised and ultimately interested drinkers from new concrete pub, shopping precinct, come out with beer to watch.

Formation dances, place-changing dances, stave-whacking-and-clanging dances, handkerchief-waving, bells-on-legs-chinking dances, sword dances, ideally accompanied by pipe and tabor but more usually by accordion. Chap dressed as hobby horse prances about, occasionally thwacking some dancer with a bladdery thing, like a Shakespearian fool. Another chap, not surprisingly, rattles a collecting box, but not what you would call aggressively.

In fact, altogether a more familiar sight this century than it was in the preceding one; some centuries since it was so familiar,

at any rate in southern England. The Lancashire Morris *did* flourish in the darkest early industrial days, and the north-east too always held on to its tradition of jigs and reels and sword dances (got to keep your wits about you in a sword dance—jump at the right time when someone is slashing it beneath your feet, remember the intertwining steps when the dancers go in and out, under and over, twisting the intricate line made by the holding of each end of swords by lines of

men, suddenly man in middle holds up, miraculously, a kind of octagonal mat of all swords woven together into one object).

But in our century, these things were dying out in many places, the modern revival dates from Christmas 1899 when Cecil Sharp, pioneer, arch-collector both of folk songs and folk dances, looked out of drawing-room window at Headington, near Oxford, where he was staying, and saw 'curious procession of men in white clothes coming up the drive'. It was the Headington Quarry Morris, led by William Kimber, one of the few who had kept it all going through changing social condi-

tions. Lifelong friendship (for the next sixty-two years, in fact) began with Sharp, as did also Sharp's endless, scientific persistence, recording old tunes and old steps before they died out with the last old codgers who knew them (and half a century before you could use tape recorder for this kind of thing). Today Cecil Sharp House, Regent's Park, is the national centre of the English Folk Dance and Song Society. And Morris dancing is alive and well.

Against a lot of odds really. They knew all about it in Shakespeare's Merry England, when it probably looked lustier and less formal than it does now (tough leg-muscles though those chaps outside the pub have):—

And, in the end being rescu'd, I have seen

Him caper upright like a wild Morisco

Shaking the bloody darts as he his bells

says York of the rebel Jack Cade in *Henry VI*, Part Two; but that wasn't long before Puritanism and the official, centuries-blighting frown on such things, people being put in the stocks or worse for lewde Morris-dancing, or even playing football, on the Sabbath. And then came the Industrial Revolution.

And then came Cecil Sharp. Various clubs began to be formed, and in 1934 six of them met and formed the Morris Ring. They were Cambridge, Letchworth (a Garden City), Thaxted, Oxford, East Surrey and (what else!) Greensleeves, so it's easy to see the kind of place the impetus came from. But it really isn't like that any more, even though the boss man of the Ring is called the Squire and they have a Recorder, and the braces many of them wear aren't called braces but baldrics (since that it what they are). Now there are some hundred clubs in the Ring, and

the thing is entirely classless. Either you like this kind of dancing or you don't, and if you do they will welcome you.

There is a strong sense of the wheel coming full circle. Between the thirties and fifties was probably the smartest time to sneer at folk dancing (or come to that, folk singing; though not if you heard the late Cecil Cope, an unknown-to-the-public teacher from Dartington Hall, holding a Wigmore Hall audience spellbound simply with unaccompanied, utterly authentic, hypnotically rhythmic singing). Then we began to realise that the newly-popular American square-dancing had the same ancestry, we discovered

do-it-yourself guitar songs.

The fact is, dancing is a thing you *do*, whether or not you ask questions about the dance. Some are articulate about it, some have theories going back to who knows what pagan rites; some have come to it through the prosaic medium of evening classes, some because of the beer, some because their fathers did it and their fathers before them. It doesn't seem to matter when you see them all at it in the Albert Hall (or outside a pub, or on the piazza by St Paul's). It's simply a matter of people coming together and doing something together, so well that it can only be achieved by months or *years* of doing it together.

All the same, some are more mysterious than others. In room 2a, just back from the pub (a good walk from the Albert Hall, but they found it all right) are the Britannia Coconut Dancers from Bacup, Lancs. Passers-by must have stared. They couldn't have guessed these men had names like Brian Daley (Gas Board supervisor), Frank Simpson (mechanic), Richard Shufflebotham (joiner) and were led by John Flynn (maintenance man, slipper factory). They have coal-black faces, showing rolling whites of eyes, and wear black jersey and breeches, clogs, white stockings, white 'kilt' more like a mini-

skirt, with narrow red bands, a white sash (over right shoulder for 'men', left shoulder for 'women'. 'You don't have women in proper Morris dancing,' says Brian Daley matter-of-factly) and a kind of white shako, with red pompom for 'men', blue for 'women'.

Their basic repertoire is five 'Garland' dances and two 'Nut' dances. They do Garland No. 2 first. Perky 6/8 tune, te tumpity tumpity tum. Curious bull-in-china-shop effect, great dolls nodding at one another, they hold 'garlands', which are wire hoops covered with paper roses, sometimes straight over heads, sometimes waved left to right as dance circles expand and contract, with changing patterns of four and four men, two and six. Music is by section from Stacksteads Band (on their visiting card it says 'available for Church Walking Days, Carnivals, Concerts, etc.').

But the Nut Dance is more basic still. The nuts aren't actually coconuts, but wooden hollowed-out discs strapped below the knees, on the wrists, and there is one on the waist, and they get amazingly unanimous castanet effects, in all kinds of rhythmic sequence, by a series of complicated arm movements as they dance, sometimes each man making his own clacks, sometimes doing a kind of pat-a-cake with another dancer.

'Morris' dancing is a corruption from 'Moorish'—and no dancers in England could look more Moorish than this. It's said that Cornishmen, who got it from Moorish pirates, brought the dance up to Bacup and the Rossendale area between Burnley and Rochdale in the seventeenth and eighteenth centuries when demand for mining and quarrying skill attracted them, but it's all guesswork from oral tradition.

Nothing vague about the steps, though, or the strength of the tradition (though the Bacup troupe are now sole survivors of four such at the turn of the century). And the year's great event is the dance from village to village on the Saturday before Easter Sunday. It can be up to fifty miles, starting at 9 a.m. 'Teks three yur to learn dance,' said one. 'I wurn't used to clogs first time, when Ah got oam me socks wur full o' blood.' They do Nuts Dance along road, Garland outside pub; they need someone to organize the beer, because 'last year thur wur such a bloody crowd of students, we couldn't get in'. They can drink all day because 'you sweat it out before the next pub'.

They've been to Arnhem, and Dublin, and the International Eisteddfod at Llangollen, and they are busy most weekends in the summer. 'It's best to be married. Dancing gets in the way of coortin', and our wives do the costumes. We practise once a week, in the Wellington in Britannia. That's a part of Bacup.'

Bacup is a part of Britannia, too. One of the more mysterious parts.

Paul Jennings

ARE YOU AN OLD BOY, OLD BOY?

FOR many generations Old School Ties were (*a*) the only permitted spot of colour in the otherwise compulsorily gloom-coloured clothes of the middle-class British male, and (*b*) a socially obligatory way of showing what school he went to and so what class he was in (or what class his new-rich father had got him into).

Now that men have pigtails and ostrich-feather jackets, and chiffon scarves casually pulled through gold rings, and flared trousers, and (for more restrained office wear) fluorescent purple three-piece suits, you'd think (*a*) would no longer be valid, and since 'class' is now a dirty word, (*b*) wouldn't count for much either.

Well, as far as ties go, the school-uniform syndrome is still with us; in fact it is spreading—there aren't only Old School Ties now, there are an increasing number of Old Organization, Old Firm, Old Everything Ties.

Go into Munday's of Irving Street, or Lewin's of Jermyn Street, and there you will find quiet library-shelves of boxes of ties (they like to have about four dozen of each in stock, although the first one I looked in—the RAF Dental Service, as it happened—was empty). There *was* a bit of a decline after the war, they say, but demand is holding steady now. As Mr James Laver, the eminent clothes-psychologist, points out, it's probably pushing it a bit to see in the tie a survival of the lady's scarf worn by her knightly champion in the lists, or of his coat-of-arms in today's school blazer badge (old school blazers, in fact any kind of blazers, are going out, it seems. Yet there is a brisk market in old school badges, so what do they put them on, if not the breast pockets of their blazers? This whole thing is full of mystery, still).

All the same, it isn't only people who were at Corpus Christi, Cambridge, (broad brilliant red and white stripes), or Old Haberdashers (from Haberdashers' Aske's School, of course), or

Old Cholmeleians (that's got you; it's Highgate School, where T. S. Eliot and John Betjeman were both once masters) that have Ties; Wellington, that military academy, may indeed have pretty well started the whole thing with rugger colours begun in 1853, and cricket colours taken from the Crimean War medal. (As Laver points out, it was really sport that released the peacock in the Briton.) But today regiments, hospitals, even Yorkshire Egg Producers and the Fauna Preservation Society have ties.

Old gentlemen from long-disbanded regiments come in practically every day, ordering a tie of the Bombay Grenadiers, or Skinner's Horse, or the Mahratta Light Infantry. Many regiments carry the colours of their full-dress uniforms into their ties. One of the most popular ('scarcely a day goes by without someone buying one') is the Royal Flying Corps. You'd have to be in your seventies to have been in this at all.

They don't sell to just anyone. Some of the boxes have little booklets inside—the official List of Members. Thus the Jesters' Club (yellow jester, on a dark blue background); you can't just have the Jesters' Tie because you know a few jokes. 'If someone comes in and asks for a certain school, and he doesn't look right, and there isn't a List of Members, sometimes we ask him a few questions.'

There's a move away from mere stripes, purely abstract after all, towards crested ties, where you can get some more literal significance into your symbols. The London Foot Hospital has what looks like a red bootee with gold wings, the theory being that you walk on air after treatment there. The London Music College has crests with two harps. The Law Society Yacht Club, with commendable humour, has silver sharks on a black background.

All history is change, and a lot of change is so complete as to amount to reversal (only in England does 'public school' actually mean 'private school'). The whole thing is curiously illustrated by our school uniforms. There is a sense, after all, in which they could be regarded as imposing an egalitarianism. If all the boys wear the same thing the richer ones can't show off, sartorially at least. As fast as schools like Eton do away with their more distinctive clothes (the 'Eton collar' itself, for instance), many State schools encourage some sort of uniform, not without the regular news story about some parent or other protesting.

But it has to be remembered that the original foundation of Eton (in 1440), was for a 'Provost, ten priests, four clerks, six choristers, a schoolmaster, *twenty-five poor scholars*, and twenty-five infirm bedesmen'; it wasn't until after the Public Schools Act of 1868 that it really blossomed out into the splendid institution for over one thousand very un-poor boys indeed that it is today.

It is not at all beyond possibility that there should ultimately be a complete return to the original concept of a place like Eton, as a school providing advantage to those who need it most, with the posh classes, if any, going back to private tutoring. Certainly we've come a long way from the automatic social acceptance of Old School Tie hierarchies which could conceive as funny the caption under an old *Punch* cartoon showing a tipster at the races: 'I ain't one o' them blokes wot kids yer 'e knows everyfink. Now I dessay the 'eadmaster of 'Arrer Collige knows one or two fings wot I don't.' Har har. Nowadays people tend to keep quiet about having been to Arrer or Eton until they're safe in the board room.

In fact, the most striking school uniform in England has a dual quality of classlessness and, somehow, of *chance*, surprise, something we forgot to change (or did we preserve it? We're not bothered, really); something very English, that recalls Chesterton's words, '. . . Shakespeare alone among the four giants of poetry is a careless writer, and lets us come upon his splendours by accident, as we come upon an old City church in the twist of a city street.'

Few things make the visitor to London or the south of England (not to mention quite a few of the natives) turn and stare so often as the occasional sight of a boy in resplendent yet marvellously dignified sixteenth-century dress—stockings, breeches, blue frock-coat with yellow lining, neckband. Even if they know this to be the uniform of Christ's Hospital School, the uninitiated tend to think 'Ha, another piece of privilege-cum-flummery'.

Well, it is a pretty exclusive school, though not in the way you'd think. It is true that about twenty of its 800-odd boys get open scholarships to Oxford and Cambridge alone every year, never mind the other universities; that many professions (especially perhaps the actuarial and accountancy world) count many Old Blues, as ex-pupils are called, among their top echelons; Lord Brock, the great heart surgeon, was an Old Blue. So were the composer Constant Lambert, the conductor Colin Davies, the BBC music chief Sir William Glock. So were Charles Lamb, Coleridge, Leigh Hunt . . .

But it's exclusive in the opposite sense to Eton. You can't get in if your parents are *rich*. The upper income limit at the moment is £2,250 a year. Entry is either by open competition, or you can be 'introduced' by a Governor. Anyone can be a Governor who gives £2,000 to the school, and he has the right to two 'presentations'—and there is a very strong tradition that the boy presented is a deserving case, not just your young cousin once removed. There are also arrangements with some local authorities, and

places for the sons of naval and RAF families. But for the sons of the rich it isn't; posh it isn't.

In fact it's the most democratic public school there is. The only distinction in dress is based not on affluence of the boy but his seniority at the school. Juniors wear narrower *girdles* (the leather belts) or *narrowies*, and it's quite a day when you get your *broadie*. When boys in other schools are in the Lower Fourth, Bluecoat Boys are in the *Little Erasmus*. Then comes the *Great Erasmus*. Then you are a *Deputy Grecian*, or *Dep*, and at 17 you are a *Button Grecian*, with silver buttons, and velvet cuffs on your coat.

Tea is *kiff*, a walk is a *spadge* a *crug* is either a friend or, as may be seen in Charles Lamb's half nostalgic, half gosh-it-was-hell essay, the end of a loaf:

. . . our *crug*—moistened with attenuated small beer, in wooden piggins, smacking of the pitched leathern jack it was poured from. Our Mondays milk porritch, blue and tasteless . . . the Wednesday's mess of millet . . .

Lamb tells fearful tales of boys put in *dungeons* for running away, of a master who would say 'Od's my life, sirrah . . . I have a great mind to whip you,' disappear to his 'lair' from which he would emerge sometime later saying '*and I WILL too*,' as well as of kindlier masters and happier moments.

Out at Horsham, Sussex, to which the school moved from the original premises at Newgate (it was founded there in 1552 by Edward VI) they keep the traditions. There is a dinner parade every day; they march in behind their famous band. Discipline is described as 'friendly but firm'. T h e r e a r e n o dungeons.

At Edgbaston High School for Girls they used to sing, to the tune of *The Vicar of Bray*

. . . and this as law
we will maintain
And this you must
confess, sir,
There is no school
in all the land
We love like
E.H.S., sir.

There are Old Girls, too. What will the ex-pupils of the proliferating comprehensives be called? Old Persons?

Paul Jennings

THE EARLY PEARLIES

BY THE time Pearly Kings had got into the national folklore, the costermongers who had developed this unique uniform were on their way out as actual traders.

In the eighteenth and early nineteenth centuries, before the railways, the wholesaling system based on the great markets, or today's road-fleets, they had a real importance as distributors, particularly of perishable foodstuffs.

Our picture of what it is that the few modern costermongers actually *do* is vague, and probably influenced by Steptoe-and-son notions of men with little carts containing nothing-in-particular. But the word comes from 'costard', which was the earliest English kitchen apple of any importance. In the old days, if you saw a man with a basket, wearing an ordinary frockcoat, and waistcoat, with blue apron, you would know he was an oysterman. If he wore jersey, breeches and fantail hat he was a fish porter. To each trade its dress; not the ubiquitous overalls of today. But even then the costermonger was rather grand.

Mayhew says 'a well-to-do coster, dressed for a day's work, wears a small cloth cap a little on one side . . . close-fitting tie-up skull-cap . . . ringlets at the temples . . . hats they never wear, excepting on Sundays, on account of the baskets frequently carried on their heads . . . waistcoats of broad-ribbed corduroy with fustian sleeves and buttoned up nearly to the throat.'

A certain gypsy-like swagger about the whole thing, in fact. They were always flashy dressers.

Another part of the dress was a neck cloth, always known as a 'king's man'. And they might buy trousers advertised as 'a pair of out-and-out fancy kicksies cut to drop down over the trotters'.

The pearly bit developed in Victorian and Edwardian times. In fact there are so many pearl buttons sometimes in patterns, sometimes covering practically every square inch and weighing up to sixty pounds, that the rest of the costume is insignificant in comparison. But by the time music-hall artists like Albert Chevalier had popularized the Pearlies, let alone the stylized (and unforgettable) Lupino Lane who made 'Doin' the Lambeth Walk' and the whole Cockney thumb-in-waistcoat image world-famous in the thirties, it had begun to take on an air of the ceremonial, not to say the showbiz, the put-on-for-tourists.

The modern functional equivalent is a 'barrow-boy', a prosaic dwindling from 'costermonger' just as 'teenager' is a prosaic dwindling from the beautiful word 'adolescent'. Modern traffic is pushing even barrow-boys off the streets, confining them mostly to static sites like the Sunday-morning market in Petticoat Lane. You can still see the Pearlies at the Derby, on Hampstead Heath at the fair (roaring amplified pop, audible from Highgate, instead of the old blooping steam-organs, though), and the Easter Monday parade in Battersea Park. But hurry; they can't get buttons any more.

Paul Jennings

...ped in the Victorian and Edwardian times. In fact there are so many pearl buttons some costumes weigh up to sixty pounds.

...y with his Lambeth joy. Dana Brown.

ERALDRY is really only romantic because it's been going on for a long time (it suddenly developed all over Europe in the thirteenth century) and all the terms are in old French-Norman. But it began as a strictly utilitarian thing. Heralds were originally carriers of messages between sovereigns and princes; they were officers at tournaments and jousts, men, with practical knowledge of arms, able to read them as a football commentator reads soccer shirts, knowing which baron was which. The shields, with their intricate rules about divisions, devices, and shapes and colours, were not only a means of identifying military units, the medieval version of uniform, but also, of course, increasingly an expression of lineage and pride of family.

Basically, the shield is divided into named areas (*dexter chief middle chief sinister base, honour point* . . .); it may be divided *per pale* (down the middle), *per fesse* (diagonally) and in many other ways; it may bear *ordinaries* (simple straight line forms such as the *chevron*, which al divide it) or common charges such as a li (in several positions, such as *rampa gardant, couchant* . . .), leopard, *dolph rose, estoile* (star); and its surface or *fi* may have a colour or *tincture* which either a colour (*gules* is red, *purpure* purple), a metal (*or* gold, or *argent*, silv or a fur. Yes, a fur—there are eight them, including *ermine* and *vair*, said to squirrel fur. Not to be confused with *v* (green). A colour must not be put another colour, only on metal or fur (e

PLAYER'S CIGARETTES

W. A. BROWN

cept that the Montmorencys were allowed to have a silver cross on a gold field, because they were the first Christians in Gaul. And don't mix the *pale* (vertical division) with the *pile* (wedge-shaped division). Then there's *differencing* for the arms of descendants, and *quartering* when arms are *marshalled* to show the union of families (have to be *re-matriculated* in Scotland. It's all different in Scotland.) And there's a whole further lot of stuff about the helmet or *crest*.

The centre of all this is the College of Arms in Queen Victoria Street. The three top chaps are Garter King-at-Arms, (Sir Anthony Wagner, a classicist), Clarenceux (Lt Col J. Walters, ex-Indian Army) and Norroy (simply means King of the North,

i.e. north of Trent) and Ulster (Mr Walter Vercoe, been in the college all his life). Then come the Heralds: Lancaster (also done it all his life), Windsor (a barrister), Somerset (was in MI5), Richmond (a historian), York (a university tutor) and Chester. The assistant, junior heralds are called Pursuivants; Rouge Dragon, Rouge Croix, Bluemantle, Portcullis.

They are in private practice (but not in Scotland, where they are salaried officials). Anyone respectable with £250 to spare can have a coat-of-arms devised (the staff of 60 includes painters and scriveners) and since a Warrant of 2 October 1961 the King of Arms has been empowered to devise arms (for instance) for any American town wanting them (and there are such).

They have around 250 new ones a year of which 75 percent are individual, 25 percent corporate.

To describe a coat-of-arms in technical terms ('*or a pile gules charged with three mullets of six points gold between as many others of the second*') is to *blazon* it. They will know at the college whether your partition lines should be *engrailed*, *invecked*, *indented*, *embattled*, *raguly*, *potenty*, *wavy*, *nebuly*, *dovetailed* or *rayonny* and much more. You can safely leave it to them. It's a pretty specialized field. As an old lady said to Richmond Herald after being shown over the college, 'It's very interesting. I had no idea you all had to be such expert gynaecologists.'
Paul Jennings

JOLLIER REGALIA

IN THE uncertain period leading up to the massive 1974 reorganization of local government in England, with its new counties, often blurring centuries-old boundaries, divided into bureaucratic 'districts' aimed vaguely at a population of 100,000 (no doubt a suitable computer figure) there was, not unnaturally, a great deal of anxiety about the continuity of civic tradition. For the first time, there seemed to be a real doubt in many places about all those taken-for-granted sights: the mayoral robe and chain and cocked hat (or, for lady mayoress, tricorne hat; now when did *that* start, there can't have been medieval mayoresses?). But what no one seemed to notice was that it's well over a hundred years now since any piece of contemporary clothing has got into the civic dressing-up box.

At the Judge's Service, today's version of the Assize Service, you may still see in many towns, perhaps three or four times a year, a procession led by sheriff (black breeches, silk jacket, cravat, buckled shoes, sword), marshal (mere frock coat), town serjeant (a kind of beadle-ish, more fancy-dress frock coat, and a top hat with gold braid round it) with the town mace, the mayor in his scarlet robe and chain, followed by the judge and his chaplain in *their* robes; often they reverse it coming out, the judge's party leading, so that he can whizz off in his Daimler to start his judging after taking formal leave of the town dignitaries at the church gate.

In other words, you will have been seeing a ceremonial formalization of the clothes worn by the upper, or at any rate richer, classes over the centuries. In fact the office of sheriff (or shire-reeve) is much older than that of mayor, since the sheriff was the representative of the king in the early, centralized Norman, no-rot-about-democracy times. It was only long after Magna Carta (1215) and the grudging twelfth and thirteenth-century granting of charters to boroughs as municipal wealth increased, that there *were* any mayors. The word is first used, even in London, in 1414.

Then, in high medieval times, as the merchants really got going, so did civic splendour. To be the leader of a craft or merchant guild often meant, automatically, to be an alderman as well (even though this word, too, means etymologically 'royal representative', not just 'older', i.e. more experienced man, as many people assume). Even aldermen had furred robes. In less contentious days, when from the voting you often couldn't tell who was on what political side, aldermen though elected by fellow-councillors for 6 years were usually there for life; recent tendencies to manipulate this for party political ends are one reason why the new Act abolished the office.

And it is no accident that even today the very name of the bodies from whom the lord mayor of London is elected—the *Livery* Companies—should denote a class who by the actual richness of their dress could show they were at the top of the tree.

It is very doubtful if many members of today's Livery Companies, for the most part stockbrokers and other businessmen, have much intimate knowledge of the trade of Loriner, Vintner, Cordwainer, Worshipful Spectacle Maker, or even Grocer or Pepperer. But they know what to *wear*. The Lord Mayor of London has six robes; black fur-trimmed, scarlet fur-trimmed, violet fur-trimmed, black and gold damask, crimson velvet reception robe, ditto Coronation robe. Most provincial lord mayors have at least two of these; the scarlet fur-trimmed and the black and gold damask.

As we have seen, later forms of fashionable dress—the breeches and coat of the eighteenth century, the frock coats and top hats of the nineteenth, have been effortlessly absorbed into the ceremonial which is surely one of humanity's ways of reminding itself that although the generations come and go, we are all part of a continuous process (and if anyone thinks that this is just a fuddy-duddy Old World, outmoded instinct, let him look at the dress uniforms of West Point, or many a less-famous American military academy).

But nothing has been *added*, no new item absorbed, since the top hat and the frock coat. Yet one of the curious effects of the local government reorganization has been that, while some ancient boroughs have lost their mayors (you had to apply for a Charter, all over again, if you wanted one), others, which have not had a mayor until now, have seized the opportunity to have one for the first time. And what does he wear? The same scarlet robe, the same cocked hat, the same chain. It all looks very much the same. But there must have been a moment, in our long history, when the first municipal uniform involving breeches was a wild innovation. 'Good heavens, a top hat!' someone must have said at a civic procession. Have we not missed a chance for silk plus-fours, or gold-braided overalls, or an ermine-trimmed anorak?

Perhaps it is just as well we have, when you think that the seal of Richmond Herald, I know for a fact, is made of *plastic*.

Paul Jennings

PAGEANTS

WHAT many people do not realize is
Pageants come in several sizes
You get some towns, they pay a professional,
He writes a script
Five hundred copies all stapled and clipped
And a specially composed Great Fanfare and Recessional.
But in our village, very luckily
We have Miss Buckley
Up at the school. Our earliest records are Plantagenet
But there was almost certainly a settlement here long before, so she's had to imagine it
And Episode One, 'The Celt and the Druid',
Is rather fluid.

Episode Two, 'The Martyr's Crown',
Deals with St Ceorfa, apostle of this region
(He has a great cathedral in our county town).
Tradition says his cell
Stood by a local spring (still called the Holy Well)
And there one day he heard 'the bruit of an advancing legion,
The din of clashèd arms, full many a brunt and striking
As peaceful Saxon strove with warlike Viking'.
They struck him down with axes, in their Viking way
But all were baptized on the following day.
One football team, in tunics and cross-gartered, looks quite Saxon
The other wears those splendid Viking helmets (made by Mrs Jackson).

The story of Sir Roger de Malpract
Is based on fact

And in Episode Three Miss Buckley shows
The weaver's child, Elizabeth, 'lovely as a rose';
The arrogant lord, as was his manner, told his steward, 'Go, get her.
No arguing—'tis my *droit*, I am *seigneur*.'
But she so prettily refused to yield
He *married* her, and gave her father land (the Weaver's Field).

Episode Four
Is all about the Civil War.
The reason for this of course is
All the girls who ride can be Cavaliers, on horses.

Miss Buckley did some very good research
On Thomas Simon, rector of our church
From 1712 to 1749.
The *Pastoral Verses* of this shrewd divine
Earned him the Title 'Rustick Virgil' from
Admirers (carpers called him 'Prosy Tom').
He praised the land, its calm unfever'd Bliss
In harmless couplets rambling on like this.

Episode Six, called 'Education'
Shows us the children of each generation.
Our village school last year was bulldozed to the ground
But we were lucky; now they come from miles around
(The 'catchment area') to our fine new Modern one
Where every dusty subject is disguised as Fun;
The children are not asked to learn, if they're not able,
A hard thing like the seven times table.

See, now they dance upon the village green
The whole cast gathered in the final scene;
This is our pageant; and, Miss Buckley, once again,
How glad we are for you it didn't rain.
Paul Jennings

HENLEY ROYAL REGATTA

THE ENGLISH will readily pay considerable sums for the opportunity of being seen with, or on the fringes of, Society. This is quite surprising, since few members of the Stewards' Enclosure are now noticeably patrician, nor are all competitors of the upper classes. *The Field* wrote as long ago as 13 July 1889: 'The curse of Henley is this picknicking, this ostentatious display of female finery . . . a sign of the luxurious selfishness of the times, exampled in a total disregard of the competitors, and in the *bon mot* uttered on a houseboat, that "the regatta would be perfect were it not for the horrid rowing men".'

But Henley remains 'a wonderfully pretty sight', partly because of the natural beauty of the Thames valley, enhanced by acres of white canvas and freshly-mown lawns, bordered with geraniums and hydrangeas, and partly because of the splendours of the British male adorned.

At Henley Englishmen are able to—and do—constantly remind us of their past glories, by sporting caps and blazers (or, in the case of bishops and some others straw 'boaters'), trimmed with blue or pink.

Henley Regatta takes place during the first week in July. This is not a particularly convenient date, from the point of view of British rowing, as it is almost at the beginning of the season, of which Henley is supposed to be the climax. However, it follows conveniently after Ascot, ensures a plentiful supply of strawberries, and fits in, or used to fit in, with Long Leave and the Eton and Harrow Cricket Match.

The late Robert Herrick, historian of Harvard rowing, wrote, 'When a race schedule for 3.03 starts, if your watch reads 3.08 you reset your watch.' So why wear one? Herrick also noted, 'At four o'clock all rowing stops for forty-five minutes, for reasons obvious to all who have been in England.'

In spite of these idiosyncrasies, Henley remains undeniably the most illustrious and successful private enterprise regatta in the world. Not long ago I asked a rowing official in East Germany, which currently dominates the international rowing scene, why they send crews to Henley, when they can gain all the experience they need, on multi-lane Continental courses at considerably less cost. 'Because,' he said, 'England is the birthplace of our sport, and Henley is its Mecca which every international oarsman should have the opportunity of visiting at least once in his career.'

Richard Burnell

6 ONE of the things there wasn't room for in this book is an organization called The Sealed Knot, several hundred people who in return for their expenses, enthusiastically re-enact famous battles, with every detail historically accurate; particularly battles of the English Civil War, which was principally between two types of men psychologically totally opposed, the Roundheads and the Cavaliers, a division still reflected within The Sealed Knot. This not only satisfies the instinct for dressing up, but simultaneously the instinctive feeling that there is hardly anything not worth preserving—whether it be old uniforms, old railways, old cars, old buildings (getting nearer our own time now; 'old buildings' includes many Victorian splendours) as well as old battles.

THE SECOND STEAM AGE

RAILWAY preservation as a movement dates from 1950, when diesel was soon to come, interesting old engines which had served gallantly through the war were being replaced by standard types, and branch lines were fading. Many people felt a real need to keep the railway past alive for future generations, and now had more time, and perhaps more money, to spend on active leisure pursuits.

The initial successes were the Welsh narrow-gauge lines; Talyllyn re-opened in 1951 (led by the pioneering enthusiasts L. T. C. Rolt and David Curwen) and Festiniog, opened in 1955. The first English, and standard-gauge, societies soon followed. In 1959 the Leeds University Railway Society saved the Middleton Railway (two miles), still the only preserved line operated primarily for freight. Now, like so many, a Trust, it opened in 1960 and was followed by the famous Bluebell Line in Sussex (Sheffield Park to Horsted Keynes) which in 1972 carried ¼ million passengers.

Since 1950 some twenty more standard and narrow-gauge lines re-opened, and now nearly a hundred miles of 'preserved' line are open to the public all over the country, with plans for a lot more. All were started by volunteer enthusiasts, but some, like

the beautiful Dart Valley in Devon (which now also runs a scheduled, year-round service between Paignton and Kingswear), and the Severn Valley (based on Bridgnorth) expect to earn a small profit for investors. Every summer weekend visitors flock to Bridgnorth station, alive with bustle, steam, smoke, uniformed attendants, bar, refreshment room, and board a puffer through superb countryside (the line will soon be extended to Kidderminster, 15 miles away).

Many groups concentrate on a particular pre-Grouping railway or class of engine. Such are the Great Western Society, with a Didcot depot capable of extensive overhaul work, and the centres at Tyseley, Carnforth and Ashford. Less grand 'living museums' are at fifteen other sites, which offer pleasant 'open days' with rides over a few hundred yards with a few wagons or an old carriage.

Co-operation between societies has been promoted by a central Association of Railway Preservation

Societies, which is able to share knowledge learned the hard way and to negotiate with authority. It was largely through the efforts of the ARPS that British Rail agreed to a 'return to steam' in which occasional steam trains could run over main lines. Since 1972 this has given enormous joy to literally hundreds of thousands of people; an added bonus for the enthusiasts who devote all their spare time to and derive endless satisfaction from working on a railway—and preserving the steam train.

John Fairman

VETERAN AND VINTAGE

MAYBE it is significant that British entry into the European Economic Community in 1973 was immediately commemorated by a mid-winter procession of veteran and vintage cars and other historic vehicles to Brussels, flagged off by the prime minister from Horseguards Parade.

The traditional English love of fettling and driving old motor cars was first made apparent as a result of a newspaper publicity stunt organized by the *Daily Sketch* and *Sunday Graphic* in November, 1927. Entitled 'The Old Crocks' London to Brighton Run', this was a re-enactment of the original London-Brighton Emancipation Run of 4 November 1896, to celebrate the passing of the Locomotives on Highways Act, which first allowed motor vehicles to be used on public highways without a pedestrian having to walk in front. It is well known that pedestrians have been walking in front of motor cars ever since, but not compulsorily.

Cars which were twenty-one years old or more were eligible for the 1927 Run, and the event was repeated in November 1928 and 1929, by which time the minimum age had been extended to twenty-five years. In 1930 the Run was organized by the Royal Automobile Club, as it has been ever since. There were fifty-nine entries received, and the age limit for the cars was set at 1904. It was after this Run that the Veteran Car Club of Great Britain was founded, as a plaque on the wall of the bar in the Ship Hotel, Brighton, testifies.

From now on the 'Old Crocks' were given the more respectable name of 'Veteran Cars', and only cars built before 1905 were accepted by the VCC as 'Veterans'. There was no particular reason for the choice of this date, except that it was felt that after 1904 motor-car design had progressed beyond the early primitive, or veteran stage.

The founding of the Vintage Sports-Car Club in 1934 came about as a result of disillusionment with the design and workmanship put into the majority of what were then contemporary motor cars. Originally motor cars which were five years old or more were eligible for membership, but by 1936 it was ruled that only cars built before 1931 were considered to be vintage. The choice of 1930 as the final vintage year was arrived at because after that date mass production really got into its stride.

As the best cars of the twenties could then be bought for a fraction of their original cost, VSCC members preferred to drive them as their every-day cars and compete with them at week-ends in trials, speed trials and races organized by their club. This state of affairs continued into the forties, fifties and early sixties, by which time modern cars had improved so much that VSCC members could admit to enjoying driving them for every-day purposes, even though their efficiency could not replace the charm and character of their cherished vintage cars.

In 1936 the VSCC instituted the Edwardian Class, for the very attractive cars, epitomized by the Silver Ghost Rolls Royce, built between the veteran and vintage periods, now recognized as 1905–18 inclusive. After 1945, the VCC extended their activities to include the Edwardian cars, and the VSCC accepted certain approved sports and luxury cars of the thirties which were encumbered with the title of Post Vintage Thoroughbreds.

Today the VSCC has over six thousand members and the VCC nearly two, with the Brighton Run annually attracting some three hundred entries. There are other smaller regional and one-make clubs (though some of the latter are as big as the VCC) and there is a four thousand strong Vintage Motor Cycle Club as well as an Historic Commercial Vehicle Club. For some years, the Department of the Environment has consulted a Joint Committee of these clubs before introducing any new road vehicle legislation, as a result of which veteran and vintage vehicles enjoy certain exemptions, although without their use being restricted in any way on the roads.

An American 'Antique Automobile Club' was founded in 1938 and today there are veteran and vintage clubs in most foreign and Commonwealth countries. However, the foreigners, on the whole, tend to be 'bonnet polishers' and do not drive their cars in the uninhibited English manner. In the VSCC the biggest crime is not to make good use of one's car, and in contrast to bonnet polishing, there is nothing the members enjoy more than racing their now valuable cars at Silverstone and Oulton Park, or trying to get them to the top of the muddiest hills in Wales or the Lake District.

An illustration of the English Difference was shown at a short 'retrospective' race for old sports cars held before the 1973 Le Mans Twenty-four Hour Race to commemorate its fiftieth anniversary. To the amazement of the French, some of the English contingent blew up their engines and ran off the road in their efforts to beat each other whilst the foreign drivers toured round. Finally the race was won by a vintage Bentley, whose driver's chagrin was acute when all he received was a toy Model T Ford while the first Frenchman to finish was presented with a large and exceedingly handsome cup.

Peter Hull

LAMBERT & BUTLER'S CIGARETTES.

A.B.C.

LAMBERT & BUTLER'S CIGARETTES.

ARMSTRONG-SIDDELEY.

LAMBERT & BUTLER'S CIGARETTES.

MORRIS-COWLEY.

LAMBERT & BUTLER'S CIGARETTES.

VAUXHALL.

LAMBERT & BUTLER'S CIGARETTES.

SINGER.

LAMBERT & BUTLER'S CIGARETTES.

SWIFT.

LAMBERT & BUTLER'S CIGARETTES.

CALCOTT.

LAMBERT & BUTLER'S CIGARETTES.

LANCHESTER.

LAMBERT & BUTLER'S CIGARETTES.

STANDARD.

LAMBERT & BUTLER'S CIGARETTES.

WOLSELEY.

LAMBERT & BUTLER'S CIGARETTES.

NAPIER.

LAMBERT & BUTLER'S CIGARETTES.

AUSTIN.

LAMBERT & BUTLER'S CIGARETTES.

SUNBEAM.

LAMBERT & BUTLER'S CIGARETTES.

DAIMLER.

LAMBERT & BUTLER'S CIGARETTES.

RT & BUTLER'S CIGARETTES.

CROSSLEY.

LAMBERT & BUTLER'S CIGARETTES.

ROVER.

TRAMS

RAMLINES were a comfortable homey spider's web holding the Edwardian town together, marking its skeletal shape. Even now in many towns you can see how far trams got. The last iron pole, from which an arm supported by a scroll-work bracket carried overhead wires, was the terminus. Already there was a hint of fields and stiles beyond the new, 1930s housing estates with their gables, and privetted, laburnum front gardens. But the trams weren't interested in the country. The conductor swung the trolley arm through 180 degrees, turned the seats the other way and with a slight groan the ambivalent vehicle, with identical myopic headlight (apparently containing a sixty-watt bulb) lurched back into town.

It went into towns more sociable than towns are now; a town which drew people to its heart with life—with theatre, usually full, markets, swarming life, naphtha flares, jostling crowds filling Saturday

streets, so the driver had constantly to stamp on the knob in the floor which clanged the bell (and which schoolboys clattering down the stairs automatically jumped on as they came down).

There were half-hearted attempts at sophisticated post-war trams with heaters, fabric seats and other fal-lals. But the basic tram had slatted seats and stern rules about spitting—the communal vehicle with which technology brought urban life

to a peak of organization before destroying it. Lucky those who remember trams with open top decks and tarpaulins for putting over your knee.

America had trams first, and they were introduced here, at Birkenhead, by an American with the beautiful-coincidence name of F. Train. And nobody had double-deckers like us. Trams only survive now in Blackpool and the Isle of Man—and on the mile of ex-quarry track at Crich, near Matlock, where the Tramway Museum Society (a thousand members, two hundred of them active, quite a lot *young*) operate forty trams, including a steam one, a Sheffield 330, a Cheltenham 21 and a Prague 180 (a gift. Getting well-known.) To Edwardian street façades they have recently added that of Derby Assembly Rooms, removed stone by stone. Volunteers; but an unequalled pool of know-how and enthusiasm if ever trams come back.

Paul Jennings

PRINTED EPHEMERA

THE ephemeral printing here shows something of the dichotomy of English design. A heavy loading of tradition is periodically counter-balanced by attempts at modernity.

The Rudge-Whitworth motor cycle and the Whiteway's Cyder posters were both designed in the same year (1926). The Rudge Four poster was designed by Horace Taylor with a mixture of design metaphors, including a trace of the Beggarstaffs and a whiff of cubism.

The Whiteway's Cyder poster was designed by Graham Simmons. In the mock seventeenth-century 'Dutch' still life, a plate of cider apples, an open 'champagne' bottle, and a much high-lighted glass of sparkling cider stand reflected on a high-

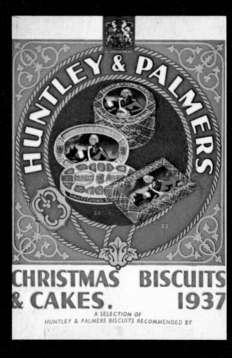

gloss Waring and Gillow fumed-oak table, in front of what looks like the top of a carved church chest. Some advertising agencies still had a firm belief in making use of the sales appeal of the English sense of tradition.

The brochure cover, 'London Aloft', produced for Gordon Hotels, and the LNER poster were designed by Victor Hicks and Austin Cooper respectively

nearly a decade earlier than Huntley and Palmer's Christmas list of 1937. The semi-abstraction of 'London Aloft' and the stylized thistle and tartans of the 'shortest-quickest' route to Scotland have given way to the biscuit-box covers of Bonnie Prince Charlie surrounded by a wealth of tartans and some abysmal typography.

Show business is often a brash business, but show people are loyal to old traditions.

The long narrow playbill format that was so popular in the nineteenth century is still used by provincial cinemas. The Plaza bill was for a cinema in a small decayed port in East Anglia. In the same year (1959) Theatre Workshop produced a bill, designed by George Mayhew, which no doubt in twenty years' time will look as dated as the Plaza poster.

John Lewis

PLAZA

CINEMA   MANNINGTREE
Proprietors: Owen Cooper Theatres.   Resident Manager: T. W. Poulter.

Monday, August 17th:

Sophia Loren - Anthony Quinn in

THE BLACK ORCHID

Ⓐ also Richard Kiley - Carmen Sevilla in

SPANISH AFFAIR Ⓐ
(TECHNICOLOR)

Thursday, August 20th:

William Bendix - Anthony Newley in

IDLE ON PARADE

Ⓐ also Pat Wayne - Dennis Hopper in

THE YOUNG LAND TECHNICOLOR

Sunday, August 23rd:

Anthony Steel, Peter Finch in PASSAGE HOME Ⓐ also
Paul Carpenter, June Thorburn in HORNET'S NEST. Ⓐ

Monday, August 24th:

Van Heflin - Tab Hunter - Kathryn Grant in

THE GUNMAN'S WALK

Ⓐ (Cinemascope and Technicolor) also Eli Wallach in

THE LINE-UP Ⓐ

Thursday, August 27th:

Kenneth More - Taina Elg in

THE 39 STEPS

Ⓤ (Technicolor) also Robin Bailey - Susan Shaw in
THE DIPLOMATIC CORPSE Ⓐ

Sunday, August 30th:

Richard Conte, Victor McLaglen in BENGAZI Ⓐ also
Virginia Mayo, Dennis Morgan in Pearl of the South Pacific
Ⓐ (Technicolor)

Monday, August 31st:

Nigel Patrick - Yvonne Mitchell
Michael Craig - Paul Massie in

SAPPHIRE

Ⓐ (Technicolor) also Peter Reynolds - Sandra Dorne in

THE BANK RAIDERS Ⓐ

Thursday, September 3rd:

Kirk Douglas - Tony Curtis
Ernest Borgnine - Janet Leigh in

THE VIKINGS

Ⓐ CINEMASCOPE & TECHNICOLOR
also THE HOMING CHINAMAN Ⓤ and Cartoon
SPECIAL SATURDAY MATINEE PROGRAMME!

Sunday, September 6th:

NO PERSON UNDER 16 YEARS ADMITTED!
Brian Donlevy, Jack Warner in The Quatermass Xperiment
(X) also John Ireland, Honor Blackman in The Glass Cage Ⓐ

Sunday, Mon., Tues., Thurs., & Sat. continuous from 5 p.m.
Wednesday & Friday once nightly at 7 p.m.

THEATRE ROYAL
STRATFORD E15

Maryland 5973

TUBE STRATFORD CENTRAL LINE
BUSES STRATFORD BROADWAY

Sat Oct 17 at 7·30 and afterwards | evenings at 8 and Saturdays 5 & 8

Theatre Workshop presents

MAKE
ME
AN
OFFER

a street-market musical by Wolf Mankowitz

lyrics and music by Monty Norman and David Heneker

produced by Joan Littlewood

THEATRE WORKSHOP
TW
A BRITISH PEOPLE'S THEATRE

MACHINES FOR MUSEUMS

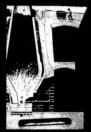

ENGLAND holds a unique place in world history -as the first country to undergo an industrial revolution. The importance of this event has long been recognized, but it is only comparatively recently that people have begun to take a serious interest in the physical remains of that revolution, the old machines and the buildings that housed them. For many, perhaps for most people, the subject was summed up for all time by William Blake's famous phrase, 'dark Satanic mills', but for the industrial historian, the remains have a unique fascination and often surprising beauty.

The Industrial Revolution was built up of a complex of changes in many different areas, but if any one place can be said to be its birthplace then that place is Coalbrookdale in Shropshire. It was here in 1709 that Abraham Darby first successfully extracted iron from its ore using coke instead of charcoal—not immediately obvious as a momentous event, but at a time when wood for charcoal making was becoming increasingly scarce, it made possible a virtually unlimited expansion in iron production. This in turn meant that iron was available for the new machines, for building and, later, for railways. The old furnace is still preserved at the Darby works, and nearby is the world's first iron bridge which was built to the design of Abraham Darby III in 1779 and crosses the Severn in a single hundred-foot span. The early industrial remains of this part of Shropshire are so important that many have been incorporated into a vast open-air museum, Blists Hill, based on the existing sites of iron-works, potteries, mines and transport links—the best possible introduction to the study of industrial history.

The next obvious step from iron-making is to the use of iron and steel, and to the city which has held its pre-eminence for centuries—Sheffield. In the south of the city is the industrial hamlet of Abbeydale, a complete eighteenth-century scythe works, in which every process can be followed from the manufacture of the steel used for the cutting edge, to the shaping of the metal under massive hammers, powered by a water wheel, and the final grinding and finishing. Also preserved there is an early furnace for producing steel in crucibles of the type developed by Benjamin Huntsman about 1742; the invention of such a furnace laid the foundations for the production of high quality steel for which Sheffield is world-famous. These crucibles were produced here and the workshop where the

clay was kneaded with bare feet prior to being made into 'pots', is still extant.

When the ingot was ready to be forged it was re-heated in a hearth in the tilt-forge where the temperature required was achieved by means of an ingenious water-driven air blowing machine for the fires. The forging then took place under the tilt hammers which were also water-driven; they were lifted by cogs on the wooden main shaft which was needed to sandwich a piece of carbon steel between an outside composed of wrought iron. The grinding machinery was driven by an eighteen-foot water-wheel and during the nineteenth century a horizontal steam engine was added to provide power in times of water shortage.

In addition to the main workshops there are a large warehouse, offices and a row of workmen's cottages. To the north of the city, at Wortley, is the even older Wortley Top Forge, where iron working began in the seventeenth century and where the huge water-powered hammers were last used in forging railway axles.

Iron was one basic material of the revolution, coal was another. Mining had, of

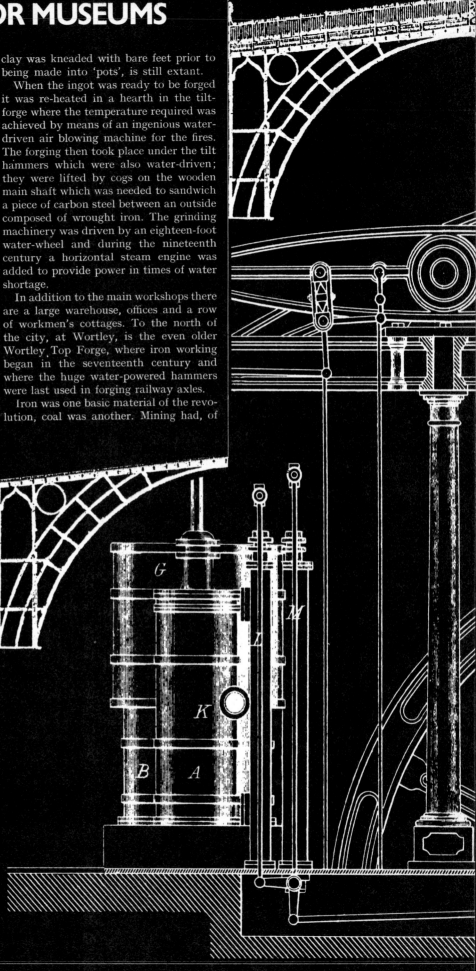

course, begun long before the eighteenth century, but deep mining depended on the ability of the miner to pump water from the workings and for deep mines this was not possible until the invention of the steam engine. The early engines worked by passing steam into a cylinder condensing it to form a partial vacuum, so that atmospheric pressure would then force the piston down into the cylinder. These atmospheric engines were very wasteful of fuel and one of the few to remain is the pumping engine at Elsecar Colliery in Yorkshire. The steam engine proper, as all those proverbial schoolboys know, was the work of James Watt who, with his partner, the Birmingham manufacturer Matthew Boulton, held a monopoly in steam-engine construction until the beginning of the nineteenth century. At Crofton, in Wiltshire beside the Kennet and Avon Canal, there are two engines, the oldest of which is a Boulton and Watt, installed in 1812. To see this great engine, which extends to the full height of its three-storey house, at work just as it worked during the Napoleonic Wars, is a rare delight. The importance of the steam engine to deep mining can be seen most clearly in Cornwall, where the engine houses of the old tin and copper mines are such a feature of the landscape. The most dramatic are at Botallack, near Lands End, where two engine houses stand in apparently impossible situations half way down the cliff face.

Of all the industries that contributed to the revolution, none showed a more spectacular growth than textiles. The northern mill towns grew to their sooty culmination in the nineteenth century, but the beginnings were set in quite different surroundings. Cromford, on the edge of the Derbyshire dales, was the site for Richard Arkwright's first water-powered cotton spinning mill; and the factories that he built here and at Matlock Bath can still be seen. Perhaps the best example of an early community built up round a cotton mill is across the Pennines at Styal in Cheshire, where the complete village—mill, shops, houses, church and the home of the apprentice children—remains much as it was almost two centuries ago.

The woollen industry was slower to develop than the cotton, but has left some of the most attractive of all industrial buildings, particularly the Cotswold-stone mills of the west of England cloth trade, centred on Stroud in Gloucestershire. The West Riding of Yorkshire is notable mainly for its large Victorian mills, but retains some delights and surprises, such as the Egyptian-styled Marshall's Mill in Leeds and the crisp Georgian elegance of the Piece Hall, Halifax's cloth market.

The industries of the time were linked by a steadily expanding and improving transport system, of which the most important part was the network of canals. Nearly three thousand miles were constructed leaving us with such remarkable engineering achievements as the 'staircase' of five locks that lifts the Leeds and Liverpool Canal sixty feet at Bingley in Yorkshire, the Anderton Lift which raises boats afloat in a 'caisson' of water fifty feet from the River Weaver to the Trent and Mersey canal and great aqueducts such as John Rennie's classical masterpiece carrying the Lancaster Canal over the River Lune at Lancaster. We have also been left the miles of peaceful waterways that today give pleasure to thousands. The railway age, too, began in the eighteenth century with horse-drawn waggons running on rails, and we can still see the Causey Arch, near Tanfield, Durham, a railway bridge built in 1727 for the local colliery railway.

Other industries have their own delights —the sinuous line of a bottle kiln in the potteries, the symmetry of a glass cone— but usually in a plain functional style. It was left to the Victorians to add a final exuberant flourish to the Industrial Revolution when they turned ordinary pumping stations such as that at Ryhope in Durham, into extravagant baroque temples dedicated to the new god of steam.

Anthony Burton

7 ENGLAND is full of societies. Her lifeboat service is provided not by the government but by the voluntary work of the Royal National Lifeboat Association. There are societies to fight cancer, leprosy, multiple sclerosis, to aid the blind, the homeless, gypsies, crippled children, distressed gentlefolk. There are societies for keeping beer preserved in proper wooden casks, for encouraging home wine-making, for performing Gilbert and Sullivan operas. There are societies for everything. The English idea of Society is one with as many societies in it as possible, serious or frivolous in aim, which you are free to join, or not. Long may it remain so.

NOT TO MENTION BRASS RUBBINGS

Obviously, anywhere in Europe the design, siting and style of the local church, from a cathedral to village level, is a major indicator, very often *the* major indicator, of history, the slow growth of culture, the evolution of style. The oldest church in Britain, the tiny St Martin's at Canterbury, has Roman tiles built into its Saxon walls, and was said by the Venerable Bede to have been used by Roman Christians. Queen Bertha, a Christian, worshipped there with her ladies, surrounded by heathens, till the day when St Augustine baptised her husband Ethelbert—tradition has it at the church's marvellous Saxon font. From such a small place came the huge flowering glory of the Cathedral down the hill. St Martin's is now, appropriately, a centre of prayer for the re-union of Christian churches.

Paul Claudel has a marvellous phrase about the replacement of the Gothic spire by the Renaissance dome; '*ce n'est plus une prière qui monte, c'est une bénédiction qui descend.*' No longer a prayer which ascends, but a blessing which descends.

That is, however, a very general observation. The special, in fact the unique glory of England's vast heritage of well over ten thousand medieval churches (there are nearer *twenty* thousand altogether) is that within this general development there is an extraordinary particularity. Partly because of a thousand years free from invasion, partly because of an unusual geological diversity in what after all is a small country (less than half the size of France) the English churches are single, individual, made of

DUNSFOLD CHURCH

local materials, often showing layers of different centuries, and always seeming an organic part of the landscape, townscape or village in which they are set. Flint churches in stoneless East Anglia, their thousand-faceted walls subtly changing colour in that clear light; austere granite churches facing Atlantic gales on Cornish uplands, stone churches in the great limestone belt reaching from the Bristol Channel to the Humber, rough-cast and rubble-and-plaster churches in Buckinghamshire, the little

flèches or spirelets known as 'Hertfordshire needles'.

Of course it is easy enough to jot down the main periods and styles. Saxon, curiously enough a lighter (perhaps because less military and fortress-like) and more vertical version of the tough Norman round arch, perhaps also remembering timber construction (you can still see an archaic Saxon timber nave at Greenstead-juxta-Ongar, Essex); and it is wicked to go through Northamptonshire without seeing the famous pilastered Saxon tower of Earls Barton. Norman itself, often surviving in churches where later additions or partial reconstructions were pointed Gothic; thus the nave, or maybe the older aisle, of many a village church, or the transepts of Winchester Cathedral, or *most* of Norwich Cathedral. Early English, the purest form of English Gothic (Salisbury, Wells, and for my money the queen of them all, Lincoln, crowning the hill and the town, drawing all that county of fen and wold to a single concentrated point as Chartres does the Eure-et-Loire cornlands). The early fourteenth-century elaboration into the marvellous intricate graceful curvilinear and geometric windows and everything denoted by the word Decorated; Patrington in Yorkshire and Heckington in Lincolnshire are famous examples; and also in Lincolnshire, St Botolph's in Boston (with the famous, visible-for-miles 'Stump'), a church which in any other county would be a cathedral; a miracle of curvilinear.

Then, after the Black Death (1350), there was a shortage of the kind of craftsmanship that had made all these glories possible. And it was from this that a peculiarly English glory was to flower: the Perpendicular, a combination of single-storeyed but lofty design, with enormous broad window spaces, in which the church was simply a 'box of light'. Since this style went on well into the sixteenth century, when everyone on the Continent was well into the Renaissance style, and since by this time there were plenty of rich merchants (very often connected with that basic English trade, wool) to endow churches—men like Thomas Spring of Lavenham, Suffolk, or John Tame of Fairford—they were jewel boxes as well. The marvellous glass at Fairford shows not only a turbulent, crimson-centred Last Judgement but all kinds of endearing detail, little out-of-perspective palaces, bits of gardens and landscape, and what is said to be the first windmill shown in stained glass.

Then we had Wren, and classicism
   . . . the walls
Of Magnus Martyr hold
   Inexplicable splendour of
     Ionian white and gold

and neo-Gothic, and 'Blue-brick Suburban' and 'Seaside High Anglican', and 'Concrete Brutalistic', everything down to 'Liverpool Cake-tin'.

But within this framework, what local glories and divergencies! Somerset is full of noble towers with crocketed corners. Kent tends to have nave and aisle under separate gables. East Anglia has not only the external glories of flint but an incredible richness of roofs.

Of course there are men who go about the country writing whole books about church roofs, or about carved screens (a peculiarly English glory), about porches, about towers, about stalls and misericords, about fonts, about pew-ends; about bells.

There is something particularly English about bell-ringing ('The Exercise', it is called by those who know). Let Continental countries play their hourly-repeated tunes, it is the English who turn the infinite mathematics of bell-harmonics and the possible combinations of the order in which a set number of bells can be rung, into an utterly distinctive and mysterious art. There are twenty-four possible changes on four bells (Singles), and they could be done in one minute. Five minutes would be needed to do them all on five bells (this is assuming each change was rung just *once*, of course; usually they do a dozen or so of each), or Doubles; and so on up to 1 day, 4 hours for the 40,320 changes (Major) on eight bells, or the 37 years 355 days a team would need to get through Maximus, the 479,001,600 changes on twelve bells. Bells keep coming into English poetry. Here is Chesterton:

And we poor men stand under the
   steeple
Drawing the cords that draw the people
And in our leash, like the leaping dogs
Are God's most deafening demagogues . . .
As awfully loaded, as airily buoyed,
Armoured archangels that trample the
   void

When bells are rung there is, over and above the individual pitches of each bell, a strange mingled hum, an infinite fusion of harmonics, a hint, something vague, indefinable. The English have never been very hot on definition, and become less so with every year that passes. Their churches may have seen zealots—Puritans, Marians, Tractarians, Evangelicals, image-breakers, image-restorers—come and go, not to mention the Dissenters who simply went, and filled the nineteenth century with bare, sometimes beautiful classical chapels. But still (especially in the countryside) England's churches, taken for granted, used for weddings, part of the landscape, reminding many of the dead and rather fewer of Resurrection, creep with a sound of far-off bells into our corporate life.

Paul Jennings

WHAT DOES THE CHEF RECOMMEND THIS EVENING, BARRATT?

HE HONOURABLE John Denzil Fox-Strangways was the son of the Earl of Ilchester: Eton, Christ Church, Coldstream Guards, a bachelor, taken prisoner in the Western Desert, a member of White's Club on one side of St James' Street and of Brooks's on the other. On the night of 24 January 1951 the late Aneurin Bevan, Labour Cabinet Minister, had been dining at White's as the guest of the Chief of Air Staff, Marshal of the RAF, Sir John Slessor. Fox-Strangways, in the bar, heard that Bevan was on the steps of the club and, though lame from a war wound, booted Bevan (to whom he had not been introduced) in the behind.

On 28 January White's issued a statement to the Press Association: 'The Hon. John Fox-Strangways, who has been mentioned in the daily editions, has resigned his membership of White's Club.' *The Times*, about the only 'daily edition' (what a splendid denigratory phrase!) which had not run the Bevan story, carried the PA item the next day.

(A short while after this episode Osbert Lancaster drew a pocket cartoon in the *Daily Express* showing two bishops and the 'Red' Dean of Canterbury on the steps of the Athenaeum. One bishop is obviously itching to kick the dean in the back of the breeches . . . is that what you wear with gaiters if you're of the cloth at that eminence? . . . and the other is holding him back. The caption is 'no, no, Fontwater. This is not White's!' White's rang Lancaster up, wishing to buy the original. But the Athenaeum had been quicker, It hangs, framed, with a number of other Lancaster originals depicting bishops in their habitat, in the lobby of that ground floor Ablutions by the lift.)

Fox-Strangways died in June 1961, aged fifty-five, and his will (over sixty thousand pounds) left £1,000 to the hall porter of Brooks's, £500 to the steward and £250 to the night porter. So, in a sense, sucks to White's on that.

P. G. Wodehouse, in his novel *Cocktail Time*, has the haughty Earl of Ickenham, a guest, I think, not a member, in the window of the Drones Club, with a catapult and a brazil nut. Unerringly he knocks off the topper (it is the first day of the Eton and Harrow match) of a pompous lawyer emerging from *his* club, The Demosthenes, across the street. If Pongo Twistleton-Twistleton, Lord Ickenham's nephew and host at the Drones, was reprimanded for this behaviour by his guest, Wodehouse deliberately conceals

the fact. I'd have thought Wodehouse and Evelyn Waugh in fiction were the last words on West End London clubs for gentlemen, though Wodehouse in fact has resigned resolutely and speedily from almost every social club his friends have made him a member of.

Evelyn Waugh was a determined club-man, Batt's and Bellamy's of his novels are roughly the White's of his diaries. In *Sword of Honour* Ian Kilbannock, failing to get into uniform at the beginning of Hitler's war, found an air marshal who longed to be a member of Bellamy's. Kilbannock put him up. Result, an immediate commission in the RAF. And

The Illustrator who

Kilbannock had taken care that the air marshal should get the necessary minimum of blackballs to prevent his being elected. As bad luck would have it, the air marshal was elected, though, and it was he, you recall, who hid cravenly under the billiard table during the air raid.

When I was young, and just starting work in London, I joined the Caledonian Club, then in St James Square. My reasons were (a) I was just Scotch enough to qualify, though not to know when to say 'Scotch', 'Scottish' and 'Scots'; (b) there was no entrance fee then and I could just afford twelve pounds a year for the sub; (c) the club had two squash courts; (d) it was thirty yards from my office, and (e) Donald McCullough, a director of my firm, wanted a steady lunchtime squash opponent. Nothing could have been more proper than the old Caledonian, or that arrangement. Yet, when I became engaged to marry a beautiful Danish girl, she and her beautiful Danish mother revealed to me that I was expected, of *course* to resign from the Caledonian when we got married. Why? I asked. It took a lot of digging out, but I found that they knew an Englishman's club was for gambling, for sulking and for getting letters and messages from other ladies. They were genuinely surprised that I didn't know that. Though I did know the legend that at Pratt's, if a wife's voice asks for a member on the 'phone, the hall porter replies 'Madam,' (or 'Your Grace' perhaps) 'no married member is ever in the club.'

Club subscriptions cannot be deducted for tax yet, I understand. Your office may pay yours as a legitimate business expense to itself and perk to you, but it is not etiquette for your office to send in one of its own cheques to the club for your entrance and sub. Some clubs frown on business documents—stock transfers, manuscripts of books, wills, plans for property development . . . being studied over meals or even in the smoking rooms. The Garrick positively forbids reading matter of any kind in the social rooms. A young actor was recently seen at the long table at lunch, conning his part before the afternoon's rehearsal, with frequent glimpses into the script in his inside breast pocket. He received, via a waiter, a reprimand from aged authority in that head prefect's armchair at the end of the table in front of the fire.

Garrick members, being conditioned, for lack of reading facilities, to chatter with each other, are regarded with some apprehension by, especially, the Travellers Club members when they are temporarily allowed to invade the Travellers during their own staff holiday. Solitary trappism (tables for one, with stands for books and papers) is among the privileges of the Travellers, who regard the Garrick lot as rowdy, and their timid 'good afternoons' at lunchtime as invasions of privacy.

Gout stools, cashing of cheques, weighing machines, betting books, no tipping, easy-come-easy-go bridge, free stationery, the inequality, if not the absence of women . . . all these survivals survive in London clubs. But problems keep cropping up in even the best-run club and even for the oldest members. Charles Graves in *Leather Armchairs* tells of the teaser that Sir John Cave set his club, the prestigious Carlton. When Sir John and his male nurse arrived from Dr Sutherland's Home for Inebriates, should the male nurse be asked to sit in the hall and wait or should Sir John be asked to give him the price of a drink and send him to the nearest pub to await a call to return to his charge? A difficult decision for the committee.

A decision that, oddly, no club has yet taken is to ask members over, say fifty-five to resign. Advanced modern thought in Clubland is that the great staircases are generally sufficient to cull membership from the top end and make room for the young. But the matter is still under discussion and clearly heart-attacks in mid-staircase continue satisfactorily in those clubs without lifts.

Richard Usborne

lked into Boodle's

BRINGING JERUSALEM

YOU sometimes hear someone say the government of this country ought to be handed over to Marks and Spencers; if they ran the country as efficiently as they run their stores we should have the Japanese panting after us trying to catch up with our Gross National Product, etc., etc. Nobody thinks to say, when searching for an image of all-pull-together efficiency, that it mightn't be a bad idea to hand over the government of the country to the Women's Institutes.

They could do worse. You'd go a long way to find an organization as efficient as the WI, both in grass-roots practical usefulness and in channelling of communications to a national centre. From the smallest green-corrugated-iron village hall to the huge annual AGM in the Albert Hall, they know how to debate resolutions without waffle, how to take the sense of the meeting, how to *get on with it*.

They have got on with quite a lot since the movement mushroomed from its beginning in 1915, when the first WI was formed in Anglesey (lots of them in Wales too, and when they come to sing the WI anthem at their meetings, Blake's *Jerusalem* they alter the words: 'Till we have built Jerusalem in *Britain's* green and pleasant land' . . . not just England's).

Anyone who has tried to get to any kind of telephone, let alone a public kiosk, in rural France, will appreciate that this is one thing we do better here; and it might not have been so if it had not been for continuous pressure from the WIs in the twenties and thirties. The same is true of rural electrification. The WIs were thinking about conservation long before it became a national issue. If the fatuous, bureaucrat's-convenience proposal to embody family allowance in tax-relief structure instead of an encashable allowance book held by the mother, as it always has been, is defeated this is largely because the ministry has listened to the WI.

Even today the Albert Hall AGM is usually good for one or two faintly sniggery or patronising pieces in various national newspapers, usually about hats. Well, it is true that so large an assembly of WI ladies *does* convey much the same comforting, so-they're-not-extinct-after-all feeling about hats that you get about flamingoes in the Camargue, or cormorants on some Atlantic rock. They may look like a mobile Chelsea Flower Show when they're coming in and out (what are they *supposed* to wear: Mao Tse Tung boiler suits and peaked caps?); but when they get down to business they have an ability to debate resolutions which

ultimately have more practical effect on the Statute Book than those of many a less decorative gathering.

Consider. They had AGM resolutions about school meals in 1926, 1939 and 1943; these were ultimately provided for by the Education Act of 1944. Their resolutions on humane killers in slaughterhouses in 1921, 1923, 1928 and 1931 (they are not easily discouraged) cannot have been without influence on the Slaughter of Animals Regulations of 1958. A resolution on the disinheriting of widows and children originally put to the AGM by the Frinton-on-sea branch in 1931 led to the Inheritance (Family Provision) Act of 1938, and a later (1966) Act has raised the 'legacy' for widows to £8,750 (recently raised by the Lord Chancellor to £15,000 (where, obviously, the estate is big enough). Secret balloting for parish council elections (1923, 1935) became law in 1956. Many of today's facts of life were once just a gleam in the eye of the AGM—things like women J.P.s (1924, 1929), women school managers (1933), and the above-mentioned rural electricity and telephone facilities. They passed a resolution condemning horror comics in 1952, and the Children and Young Persons (Harmful Publications) Act became law in 1955.

They would not claim to be the prime movers in all these cases. But they are an articulate, corporate voice, and they can certainly claim to have pioneered many good things. For the European Architectural Year of 1975, they hope to produce 'since we are in a unique position to do this, a catalogue on a national scale of places and things of historical interest and beauty—often quite small things— while there is still time for them to be noted and protected.' It is all a long way from mere pressure-groupism and the shriller forms of Women's Lib—from which, as a matter of fact, Miss Sylvia Gray, the National Chairman, took good care to dissociate the WI movement at the 1974 AGM.

These corporate decisions flow naturally from over nine thousand WIs, with ½-million members, though in fact the WIs do not exist primarily to exert political pressures, but to enhance and broaden the social life of their communities. Modern mobility has meant a breaking-up of the old watertight division between 'urban' and 'rural' people; many young families make the decisive move in their lives and settle in a village from which the father may commute miles to work in a city (or there may be a brand-new factory doing something terribly sophisticated with semi-conductors on the edge of a small old market town); and for the newcomers the way into the community, via the wife,

may very well be the local WI.

WI markets encouraging home-grown food and regional recipes, return over £500,000 yearly to small-scale gardeners with a surplus. The basic monthly meeting is usually enlivened by a lecture, by someone with something interesting to say, from a list of speakers maintained by the County Federation, and they also have available 'Programmes by Post'— recorded talks illustrated by slides.

Sometimes a WI will take on a specific village task; there are many villages where some grassy space becomes a miracle of thousands of daffodils or crocuses in spring. Some WIs have special links with neighbouring ones set up in mental institutions. Some make a particular thing of care for old people. But there are also an enormous number of ways for the ordinary member to come out of her traditionally reticent country shell. Among the National Federation Sub-committees some, such as the Public Questions and Countryside or the International, look outward. Others, such as Crafts, Speech and Drama or Music, look inward to the members, providing them with professional instruction. The WI Drama Certificate now exempts those who hold it from part of a national examination for drama teachers.

In 1965, the movement's Golden Jubilee year, there was a national competition for a scrapbook showing a year of village life. In the 2,600 entries there was an incredibly high standard of research and information about life in the country today, dialect, customs, farming, history, change, nature (often beautifully illustrated with paintings or photographs). Many of the best of these books have found their way into county libraries where they are rich material for thesis-writers.

There is a great deal more to the WIs than ladies in hats shrilly echoing Blake's
  Bring me my bow of burning gold,
  Bring me my arrows of desire;
  Bring me my sword—oh, clouds unfold!
  Bring me my chariot of fire—
and then getting on, in happy anti-climax, with the business of making jam—an extraordinarily persistent image which grew when they were asked to take over communal jam making during the war. The war has been over a long time now, and recently the WIs took another step forward when the rule about not discussing religious or political matters was rescinded. They say it hasn't, in effect, made much difference. The kind of things the WIs are interested in—children, family, the country, getting the most out of life, aren't controversial; they're just *good*.

Paul Jennings

PET THEORIES

CURIOUSLY enough, it is probably a mistake to think that the English are particularly soppy about animals.

It is true (and someone points this out in print at least once a week) that we have the *Royal* Society for the Prevention of Cruelty to Animals and only the *National* Society for the Prevention of Cruelty to Children. It is true that there is a dog cemetery in Essex where one headstone of Italian marble cost a dog-owner, a Lloyds broker, two hundred pounds. It is true I myself once saw a woman outside Harrods (where else?) with a dog that had on one of those dog coats, grey with red binding, more like a blazer really; there was a hole for the dog's tail which popped out from under the hole every time it wagged, and she kept stooping to put it in again. It is true that we spend £130 million a year on pet foods, 0.7 per cent of the income of every family in the country (and therefore a great deal more for some). But America can outdo us in this respect, as in some others. Kathleen Szasz, in a splendid book called *Petishism*, tells of the Bide-a-Wee Home Association Inc., which offers a pension plan for aged dogs and cats, and of the woman who gave a coming-of-age party (3 years, equivalent to a human twenty-one) for her dog, at which the guests, twenty-nine other dogs, started off with strawberry-flavoured milk, soup with sherry, and went on to God knows what: the dogs wore bow ties, white-fronted black jackets, and lace-up patent leather boots, and the bitches, if

that is the word, wore brocade, velvet or sequined evening jackets with matching panties and bootees.

No, there is something more subtle in our relationship with our pets. Just as England is the only European country where there have been no *peasants*, picturesque but unproductive chaps with sickles, for 150 years, but has more gardens per capita than any other country, we have *kept in touch* with nature.

Animal-consciousness shows in our literature, at all levels, from children's stories upwards. The old fairy tales, whether folk or Grimm or Andersen, featured the occasional talking animal, but the main protagonists were people, whether princes, millers' sons or goose girls. But today the characters likely to be encountered by the English-reading child are first the little animals of Beatrix Potter and then a bear called Winnie-the-Pooh. This work has been translated into Latin (*Winnie Ille Pu*), and so, for that matter, has *Peter Rabbit* ('*mox Petrus sternuit—"Kertyschoo!" Dominus McGregor eum brevissimo tempore petebat*'. 'Presently Peter sneezed—"Kertyschoo!" Mr McGregor was after him in no time'); and many others, including of course *Alicia in Terra Mirabili*. There is a brilliant translation into French, by Francis Steegmuller, of Edward Lear's *The Owl and the Pussy-Cat*:

The Owl and the Pussy-cat went to sea
In a beautiful pea-green boat,
They took some honey, and plenty
 of money,
Wrapped up in a five-pound note

becomes

Hibou et Minou allè-
 rent à la mer
Dans une barque
 peinte en jaune-
 canari
Ils prirent du miel
 roux et beaucoup
 de sous
Enroulés dans une
 lettre de crédit
and goes on equally felicitously.

Cats, of course, go very well with literature, especially *our* literature. Everyone who has read Boswell, or even just the *Oxford*

Dictionary of Quotations, knows that Doctor Johnson had a cat called Hodge, to whom he gave oysters, and 'I observed he was a fine cat, saying "why yes, Sir, but I have had cats whom I liked better than this"; and then, as if perceiving Hodge to be out of countenance, adding, "but he is a very fine cat, a very fine cat indeed"'.

And of course there is the marvellous cat-poem written in the eighteenth century by poor mad Christopher Smart, beginning 'For I will consider my Cat Jeoffry', and going on like an extraordinary surrealist psalm, every line beginning with the word 'For', ending

For his ears are so acute
 that they sting again.
For from this proceeds
 the passing quick-
 ness of his attention.
For by stroaking of
 him I have found
 out electricity.
For, tho he cannot
 fly, he is an ex-
 cellent clamberer.
For his motions
 upon the face of
 the earth are
 more than
 any other
 quad-
 rupede.
For he can
 tread to all the measures upon
 the musick.
For he can swim for life.
For he can creep.

No wonder Britten included it in the poetry by Smart which he set for his sparkling Festival Cantata, *Rejoice in the Lamb*.

The most splendid, imperious, disdainful-looking cat in the world is a Long-Haired British Blue. T. S. Eliot wrote of more demotic cats in that great *jeu d'ésprit, Old Possum's Book of Practical Cats*. In fact there is a sense in which one could say that the whole middle field of realistic literature lies between two extreme poles of allegory—sunny in *Alice in*

PLAYER'S CIGARETTES

HOUND

"HIS MASTER'S VOICE"

Wonderland (full of animals, beginning with a White Rabbit) and despairing—Orwell's bleak *Animal Farm*.

We have kept in touch with animals, we've never really let them out of our consciousness, however citified we became. You can see the whole process in the case of the Sealyham, now a white, small and perfectly bone-headed domestic dog. I had one with a pedigree as long as your arm, its uncle was Princess Margaret's dog, but we had to get rid of it in the end. After six, nay eleven, months of intense effort we finally got it to understand that there was a difference between Outside and Inside, but it got it wrong, and when it was outside it would come *in* to the house specially to make a mess.

Well, Sealyhams were once literally very bloody dogs. Sealyham was a house near Haverfordwest, in Pembrokeshire, which although it is in Wales is really very English (if you call the Normans English. They got right up there; after all, look at St David's Cathedral), and this was where a Captain John Edwardes, who really hated badgers and foulemarts (or polecats), crossed the native Corgi with some very rough terrier indeed to produce the blunt dog which was not afraid to go down a dark tunnel and massacre anything it found there. Anything, not just rabbits, but these foulecats, or polemarts.

Now, the Sealyham is a sedate town dog, looking very much like the white dog in the advertisements for Black and White Whisky (although that is actually a West Highland White Terrier). There is another one very much like it called a Cairn. This was originally used for driving foxes out from cairns (which are, of course heaps of stones). You see? All that blood, that hunting, that natural life with dogs on the land, has been gradually transformed just as public life was transformed when the vote broadened down to propertyless

eighteen-year-olds, flogging, hanging and the treadmill gave way to suspended sentences and the probation service (no doubt not so thoroughly as in Scandinavia, but then it was altogether a more organic, unselfconscious, unthought-out process).

But the animals were with us all the time. We *talk* to them. I once heard a woman say to her dog 'Come along darling, or we shall be late for lunch'. We name our products after them. The most famous gramophone trade-mark in the world, even in these days of fi so hi that addicts are disappointed by any real live orchestra, is still that dog listening to His Master's Voice. The Cerebos salt tin still shows a boy running after a bird with the legend 'See how it runs'. Even now, Guinness is still associated in the public mind with toucans (and it isn't all that long since their export stout bore brand names such as Dog's Head, Cat, Griffin, Flamingo). The word Babycham makes the best of both worlds by suggesting the sound of champagne and showing visually, in its trademark, a somewhat Disney-ish chamois, all smiling.

The old mystique of hunting and fighting has been replaced by a mystique of the show and the competition, of breeding. It's no good trying to breed dogs nowadays if you don't know things like this:

$X_H H_h$	mates with	$X_H Y$
Carrier		Normal
Female		Male

giving

$X_H X_H$ $X_H X_h$		$X_H Y$ $X_h Y$
Normal		Normal
Carrier		Haemophiliac
Females		Males

and it is a good thing to know that a Setter's tail is its flag, a dudley nose means a yellowish one, cloddy means stoutly built, and cobby just the opposite.

And just in case this should all seem too redolent of ultra-domesticity with too many of those indoor, in-bred, shivering and yapping toy dogs, let us not forget that the most popular breed at the Kennel Club is the Alsatian, and it says in the *Complete Dog* that 'no win has received more vociferous public acclaim than in 1970 when Mr and Mrs White's Alsatian *Hendrawen's Nibelung of Charavigne* was the winner'.

Nor should we forget the horse. You still see the odd *man* on horseback but now our equestrianism descends via thousands of pony-riding girls (who as mothers will hand it on). After all, it did lead to a royal marriage.

Paul Jennings

THE QUEEN

NQUIRING how one of his students was getting on with her novel, an American professor of creative writing was told 'Oh, I've practically finished it. I'm just putting the symbols in,'—so said a paragraph in the *New Yorker* some years ago.

The Queen of England (and still, at the time of writing, of Scotland, Wales, Northern Ireland, Canada, Australia, New Zealand and technically, at least, a long list of Commonwealth countries from Barbados to Zambia, who if they do nothing else at least send competitors to the Commonwealth Games) is a classic example of a symbol which doesn't need to be put in, having existed for more than a thousand years. The form and order for the British Coronation service perpetuates a tradition directly traceable back to Egbert, King of Wessex (800–36).

The Investing with the Armill and the Royal Robe; the Delivery of the Orb; the Investiture *per Annulum et Baculum* (that is, by Ring and Sceptre)—and, perhaps above all, the Anointing—go back much further, to Biblical times, when *everything* was symbolic, everything in the physical world was suffused with spiritual meaning (whereas who ever heard of a spiritual motor car?). The Coronation Stone, so dramatically stolen and recovered in the fifties, is *Lia Fail*, the Stone of Destiny, traditionally the pillow of Jacob, carried to Ireland in the fifth century B.C., thence to Scotland, thence to England by Edward I (which of course is why the Scots pinched it back). The kings of Israel and Judah were anointed with oil by the high priest; Solomon was anointed by Zadok: and 'Zadok the Priest', one of the most majestic of all Handel's anthems (which is saying something), is a traditional part of the service.

The Coronation service begins with trumpets and the thrilling treble cry of 'Vivat! Vivat! Vivat!' from the boys of Westminster School. Towards the end of the marvellous heraldic dance, moving all but the most curmudgeonly and unromantic materialist, there is that heartstopping stillness that always comes at the end of the '*Te Deum*', the sudden gear-change from triumph and joy to the muttered whisper—'*non confundar in aeternum*' it is in the Gregorian setting, 'let me never be confounded' in the usually specially-composed new version (William Walton for the present Queen, Vaughan Williams for her father). A holding of the breath; a reminder of eternity. Then time and history start again. The appearance at the West Door; bells, trumpets, guns, cheers.

And television cameras. She is a Queen in a world where many people are faintly embarrassed even by the symbolism inherent in the words 'with this ring I thee wed, with my body I thee worship'. A world where MPs with rather tight lips ask questions about how many bathrooms there are in the royal yacht. A world where royalty marries businessmen or photographers, and in which the Queen herself has to appear on the most dehumanizing of things, the television.

It cannot be an accident that just when industrial materialism was really taking over western civilization there was a movement in poetry, actually *called* Symbolism, which led to T. S. Eliot and is still a main root of such creative writing today as is not merely historical, political or pornographic. Obviously there is a fundamental human need for some kind of symbol.

Equally obviously, for lots of people in the age of astronauts and atom bombs, there is tension, contradiction, perhaps even direct clash, between a symbolism that goes back to Solomon, and the flat, unsymbolic world of plastics and the transistor radio (a magic box not magic because taken for granted).

It's not surprising that this comes out fairly strongly in foreign reactions—not necessarily hostile, although they can be very bitchy, even if not up to *Private Eye* levels. One issue of *Paris-Match* patiently followed Prince Charles on his first ski-ing lesson and simply printed all the pictures that made him look like Marcel Marceau impersonating the Spirit of Awkwardness. On the other hand they said of Princess Anne's wedding that 'hers was a throne surrounded by the panache of plumed helmets, of gilded carriages, of caparisoned grey horses, of ranks of scarlet halberdiers . . .'.

Le Monde had a three-hundred-word story headed *Un Beau Mariage*—but it was all about the wedding of an accountant and a punch-card operator at the *Mairie* of the 10th *Arrondissement* in Paris, while an immigrant worker was seeking social security in the next room; and underneath this there was a straight account (250 words) of the royal event.

But of course what really fascinates all commentators is the personal lives of these symbols, an obsession sometimes bordering on the fatuous ('do you take *money* with you when you go shopping?' asked one television interviewer. 'O, yes, you'd be surprised what we get up to,' replied Princess Anne. Forty-love to her, that was.) I remember a splendid story, also in *Paris-Match*, about some young scion of the nobility who was squiring Princess Alexandra, before she married Mr Ogilvy. His ancestors, they said, had fought at *la*

bataille de Flobben and after following them round for the whole evening the report said that she invited him in for a few moments '*avec l'invitation traditionelle anglaise*: "have a night cup, old chap".'

And of course there is always the famous *France-Dimanche*, which Sunday by Sunday runs an entirely fictitious royal soap-opera. *Elizabeth et Philippe séparés!* said one poster I saw (he was at Cowes, she was at Balmoral).

But there is probably an even greater amount of sympathetic than unsympathetic reporting. At home the confusion between the Queen as a person and the Queen as a symbol is getting more complicated as the classless society recedes ever further into the future while the universal pap of the media becomes ever more inescapable. It is more complicated now than it was, for instance, when G. K. Chesterton was delighted to see a street poster in the East End during the Silver Jubilee celebrations for George V, saying 'LOUSY BUT LOYAL'. Divinity doth hedge a king, wrote Shakespeare; but that was Hamlet's uncle trying to justify his usurpation by invoking medieval certainties. In the good old days, once you *were* the anointed Symbol it didn't much matter whether you were a saint, a nephew-murderer, a madman or a homosexual (we've had them all). But by the time James I was having to spell out the Divine Right of Kings we were on the way to the monarch who 'reigns but does not rule'.

Yet something, a faint gleam, a residual magic remains, even though the Queen be represented on our stamps by what appears to be an old daguerrotype of Shirley Temple. A lot of radical chaps say the whole thing is outmoded, but they can be seen wiping away the furtive tear when there is some big royal occasion on the telly, and there are probably lots of people who (like me) would like it compulsory for heralds and kings-at-arms, if they can't see without glasses, to wear contact lenses, not horn-rimmed glasses, with their splendid medieval tabards.

In fact the English are very good at ambivalence. It is not totally impossible that the Coronation service will be altered; *then, the Chrism having been poured by the Secretary of the British Humanist Association, the Orb shall be presented to the Archbishop by the Unknown Miner . . . a fanfare being sounded, the Monarch shall present himself to the People at the West Door. Twelve Armature Winders, being Members of the Electrical Trades Union, shall then bring forth the Golden Bicycle of State . . .*

Whatever they do, a lot of it will still go back to Solomon.

Paul Jennings

Page and title of Article		Artist	Writer
10	The Lie of the Land	Bob Priest	W. G. Hoskins
12	Wild, on the Island	Anna Pugh	Dr Max Hooper
14	All the Fun of the English	Geoff Weedon	Geoff Weedon
16	Accustomed as we are	Homer Sykes	Paul Jennings
18	Local Architecture	Michael Dempsey	Paul Jennings
20	Water	Homer Sykes	Miles Hadfield
22	Country Town	David Gentleman	G. Ewart Evans
24	The Village Fête	Paul Leith	Paul Jennings
26	Writers' Regions	Dick Weaver	Paul Jennings
28	All Kinds of Gardens	Neil Davenport Joyce Tuhill	Xenia Field
32	Gardening Folk Figures	Larry Learmonth	
34	Grow It Yourself	Dick Weaver	Paul Jennings
38	Whatever Happened to Fang Managers?	Adrian George	Paul Jennings
40	Anyone for Yealming?	Graham Evernden	Paul Jennings
43	Unite in Love	Tony Evans	John Gorman
46	Brass Bands: at Work and Play	John Gorham	Violet Brand
48	On the Company's Ground	Keith Bowen	George Torkildsen
52	Top of the Bill at the Mechanics' Institute	Bob Lawrie	Paul Jennings
56	Interior Recollection	Howard Brown	Paul Jennings
58	Shall I Wrap It Up?	Larry Learmonth	Paul Jennings
60	Meat and Drink to Us	Alan Cracknell	Paul Jennings
62	Now there are Plenty of Teaspoons	David Hillman	Paul Jennings
64	U'd Be Surprised	Ann Winterbottom	Paul Jennings
68	Popular Pleasures	Michael Farrell	Paul Jennings
70	Huntin', Shootin' and Fishin'	Neil Davenport	Paul Jennings
72	Odder Games	George Hardie	Paul Jennings
74	Come Out to Play	Tony Meeuwissen	Paul Jennings
76	The Lyke Wake Walk	Keith Bowen	Paul Jennings
78	The County Show	James Lloyd	Paul Jennings
80	The Sporting Weekend	Michael Foreman	Paul Jennings
82	Something about a Dame	Peter Rauter	Paul Jennings
84	On, On, On with the Dance	Brian Love	Alex Moore
86	Pop	Bush Hollyhead	Chris Welch
88	Make Mine a Pub	Harry Peccinotti	Paul Jennings
92	O, I Do Like	David Pocknell	Paul Jennings
96	Singing is so Good a Thing	Peter Rauter	Paul Jennings
98	The Casual Look	Arthur Robins	Paul Jennings
102	The Haxey Hood Game	Peter Rauter	Paul Jennings
104	Bacup, and Other Dancers	Bill Tidy	Paul Jennings
106	Are You an Old Boy, Old Boy?	Alan Fletcher	Paul Jennings
108	The Early Pearlies	Donna Brown	Paul Jennings
110	Argent Threads Among the Or	Brian Love	Paul Jennings
112	Jollier Regalia	Roger Law	Paul Jennings
114	Pageants	Brian Love	Paul Jennings
116	Henley Royal Regatta	Arnold Schwartzman	Richard Burnell
120	The Second Steam Age	Ken Carroll	John Fairman
122	Veteran and Vintage	Ken Carroll	Peter Hull
124	Trams	Ken Carroll	Paul Jennings
126	Printed Ephemera	John Lewis	John Lewis
128	Machines for Museums	John Gorham	Anthony Burton
132	Not to Mention Brass Rubbings	John Gorham	Paul Jennings
134	What Does the Chef Recommend this Evening, Barratt?	Peter Brookes	Richard Usborne
136	Bringing Jerusalem	David Pocknell	Paul Jennings
138	Pet Theories	John Gorham	Paul Jennings
140	The Queen	Lou Klein	Paul Jennings

Professor W. G. Hoskins, CBE, FBA
is the pioneer of the modern school of British local history studies, which he began as a
Lecturer at Leicester University, returning to the Chair there in this new subject
after a spell as Reader in Economic History at Oxford. His two best-known
books are the famous *Local History in England* and
The Making of the English Landscape.

Dr Max Hooper,
an ecologist for twenty years, Secretary of the Northamptonshire Naturalists' Trust, works
for the Nature Conservancy, and is the discoverer of a method of dating old hedges by
counting the number of species in them.

Geoff Weedon
is an advertising art director who has made a special study of fairground
decoration and tradition.

Miles Hadfield,
born in a 1795 house with a lake and trees, says 'I have been a gardener all my life'. He
holds the Gold Medal of the Royal Forestry Society.

George Ewart Evans,
author of *Ask The Fellows Who Cut The Hay* and several other books on rural
life and tradition, is a Welshman who moved to East Anglia, where he has also pioneered
research into oral traditions.

Xenia Field, MBE
is Gardening Editor of the *Daily Mirror*. She is also a Justice of the Peace
and ardent prison reformer.

John Gorman
is a printer, author of *Banner Bright* and organized an exhibition of Trades Union Banners
at the Whitechapel Art Gallery in 1973.

Violet Brand
is the wife of Geoffrey Brand, conductor of the Black Dyke Mills Band and Editor of
The British Bandsman.

George Torkildsen
is Director of the Harlow Sport centre.

Alex Moore
is Chairman of the Imperial Society of Teachers of Dancing, President of the International
Council of Ballroom Dancing, and author of *Ballroom Dancing*.

Chris Welch,
after general journalism turned to writing about pop music, on which he now has a wide
following as Features Editor and writer on *Melody Maker*.

Richard Burnell
is rowing correspondent of the *Sunday Times*.

John Fairman
is an engineer, and Editor of the Bulletin of the Quainton Railway Society (which incorporates
the London Railway Preservation Society).

Peter Hull
is Secretary of the Vintage Sports Car Club and author of several books on old cars, including
Alfa Romeo: A History, and *The Vintage Alvis*.

John Lewis,
book designer, editor, author and typographer, has taught at the Royal College of Art and is
still deeply involved in art education. Works include *Printed Ephemera*, *Anatomy of Printing*
and a monograph on *Heath Robinson*. In progress: *Collecting Printed Ephemera*.

Anthony Burton
has done many jobs, from publisher's editor to railway porter. Works include *The Canal
Builders*, *A Programmed Guide to Office Warfare*, *The Reluctant Musketeer* (about
national service) and *Remains of a Revolution*.

Richard Usborne
is the author of *Clubland Heroes* and *Wodehouse at Work*.

Paul Jennings (centre)
was born in 1918 in Leamington, grew up in Coventry where he went to King Henry VIII School; at 15 he
transferred to Douai School where the headmaster, Dom Ignatius
Rice, was a personal friend and admirer of G. K. Chesterton. At 18 he answered
an advertisement for 'young men with Higher Certificate to train as radio engineers', at the
General Electric Company, Coventry, and was into the job, dropping expensive valves
and blowing out expensive ammeters, before they really took it in that his Higher Certificate was in
Latin and Greek, not Physics and Maths. This partly explains why he ended his war service as a lieutenant
in the Royal Corps of Signals in India. He got freelance work accepted by *Punch*
while still in the Army, but his first post-war
job was writing film strips about British carpets, British ball-bearings,
British schools, British everything, for the Government's Central Office of Information.
After a brief spell in advertising, in 1949 be became the *Observer's* first humour columnist, with
his feature *Oddly Enough*, which
(decanting it into twelve books) he wrote till
1966. He has also written a history of Dunlop; a picture
of English rural life based on the pick of 2600 Women's Institute Scrapbooks called *The Living Village;*
a study of four disused railway lines called *Just A Few Lines;* and three children's
books. He is married to Celia, daughter of the late Eric Blom, music
critic, sings in the New Philharmonia Chorus,
and has six children. He now writes
articles for the *Telegraph Magazine*, reviews books for the *Sunday Times*,
broadcasts in radio and TV panel games and does things like this book.

John Gorham (right)
born in 1937, went to a secondary modern school in Uxbridge, and after a
spell at Harrow (the Art School, not the posh one) worked as an apprentice at the Silk
Screen Company, then worked as a designer first in the publicity department of the *Daily Mirror*, later in
the marketing department of the *Sunday Times*, then as Art Director at
Cassons Advertising Agency. The New York Museum of Modern Art has two of his
posters in their collection and he has won many awards, including
those of the Council of Industrial Design and
Communication in Arts (USA). He has done many book jackets, including those for the
Penguin editions of Scott Fitzgerald. He now runs his own design business
and teaches one day a week, at the
Royal College of Art in London. He is married, loves looking at and photographing
'average homes and shops', playing cricket (which he used to do for Uxbridge), collecting cigarette cards
and children's books.

Ken Carroll (left)
born in 1946 in Pentre, South Wales, went to a total of thirteen
schools throughout England and the Far East. He studied graphics at the
London College of Printing and started as an illustrator and designer with the *Financial Times*. He
went on to join BPC as a designer with Germano Facetti on *History of the*
20th Century and later as Art Director of two publishing houses before starting his own design
business. He now freelances in the whole field of
magazine and illustrated book design from the
jacket inwards for Penguin, Fontana, Macmillan and many
others. Married with one child and two cats, he lives in Dulwich and is an avid filmgoer and
collector of bygones, particularly tobacconists' bygones.